Florida's
Haunted
Hospitality

Michelle Davidson

4880 Lower Valley Road • Atglen, PA 19310

Schiffer Books are available at special discounts for bulk purchases for sales promotions or premiums. Special editions, including personalized covers, corporate imprints, and excerpts can be created in large quantities for special needs. For more information contact the publisher.

Published by Schiffer Publishing, Ltd.
4880 Lower Valley Road
Atglen, PA 19310
Phone: (610) 593-1777; Fax: (610) 593-2002
E-mail: Info@schifferbooks.com

For the largest selection of fine reference books on this and related subjects,
please visit our website at:
www.schifferbooks.com.
You may also write for a free catalog.

This book may be purchased from the publisher.
Please try your bookstore first.

We are always looking for people to write books on new and related subjects.
If you have an idea for a book, please contact us at:
proposals@schifferbooks.com.

In Europe, Schiffer books are distributed by
Bushwood Books
6 Marksbury Ave.
Kew Gardens
Surrey TW9 4JF England
Phone: 44 (0) 20 8392 8585; Fax: 44 (0) 20 8392 9876
E-mail: info@bushwoodbooks.co.uk
Website: www.bushwoodbooks.co.uk

Other Schiffer Books on Related Subjects:
Florida Ghosts & Pirates: Jacksonville, Fernandina, Amelia Island,
St. Augustine & Daytona, 978-0-7643-3020-9, $14.99
Hauntings in Florida's Panhandle, 978-0-7643-3134-3, $14.99

Cover photograph courtesy of John Roppolo.
Designed by Mark David Bowyer
Type set in Artistik / NewBaskerville BT

ISBN: 978-0-7643-4120-5
Printed in the United States of America

Contents

━━━

This book is dedicated to the spirit known as Lavender. She reached out to tell me her story and provided me the signs that I should research and write this book. She started me on this journey of spiritual awareness — and for that, I will be forever grateful.

━━━

Acknowledgments

Special thanks to all of the innkeepers who gave me the opportunity to stay at their inn. Thanks for the wonderful hospitality, stories, and haunting experiences.

Thanks to Apollo Paranormal, Big Bend Ghost Trackers, and Southern Ghosts, for expanding my knowledge of the paranormal.

Thanks to all the ghost tours that enlightened and entertained me with local ghost legends. And finally thanks to all the people and spirits that have shared their stories with me and made *Florida's Haunted Hospitality* a reality.

Introduction

Over the past five years interest in the paranormal has grown due to television shows, books, the Internet, and investigation groups and tours. Where it once might have been taboo to talk about the subject of spirits, people are becoming more aware of paranormal occurrences in the mainstream.

In the State of Florida, the towns not only cherish their history, but they are also aware of and even promote its paranormal history. St. Augustine is one such city in Florida that has made haunted hospitality a seat of entertainment and insight. Ghost tours and investigations thrive there, and just about every local and business owner has a ghost story to tell. If you have an interest in history and are looking to experience a paranormal occurrence firsthand, immerse yourself in Florida's haunted hospitality.

Whether you go on a ghost tour, investigation, or stay the night at one of Florida's haunted inns, you have the chance to be enlightened as to what is possible in the realm of the paranormal, but before you set out on your adventure, it is a good idea to know the basic theories of the paranormal.

Every culture has its own beliefs concerning the afterlife. While there are several theories about what ghosts and spirits are, *Merriam Webster's Collegiate Dictionary 10th edition* defines a ghost as:

1. The seat of life or intelligence
2. A disembodied soul, the soul of a dead person believed to be an inhabitant of the unseen world or to appear to the living in bodily likeness
3. Spirit, demon
4. A false image in a photographic negative. With this definition, many Americans claim to have had an encounter with the paranormal at least once in their lifetime.

According to the ghost-hunting group Big Bend Ghost Trackers (BBGT), there are three types of ghosts: *interactive*, *residual*, and *non-*

human spirits. Interactive spirits may act similar to the living with their five senses, as they can communicate through voice, noise, odors, temperature changes, and touch. Interactive spirits are varied in how they use their energy to manifest: they could appear as full or partial apparitions, shadows, light sources, or orbs. There are also several cases where spirits can communicate through telepathic or dream precognition. Residual hauntings are non-communicative. The event, scene, or apparition acts out a moment in time that is traumatic, eventful, or emotional over and over again. In rare cases, there may be a non-human spirit, known as a demon; these are often considered harmful or evil to some.

There are several theories as to why spirits remain earthbound. Betty Davis, the founder of BBGT, believes "that spirits that walk the earth have a message to tell before they can move on." Spirits can be aware they have passed on and still choose to stay behind to take care of unfinished business with loved ones or relay a final message to someone. Other spirits may be unaware that they are dead due to an unexpected tragic death. These spirits don't know how to cross-over. A spirit's fear or guilt can also cause them to stay earthbound. It may be hard for a spirit to go to the next level if they cannot communicate with the living or come to terms with their death. They may need to rely on our energy and openness to help them.

Spirit communication can vary with different people. Psychics and mediums can communicate with spirits; they can also sometimes sense and see events that happened in the past as well as the future. Sensitive people who are attuned to the paranormal feel the emotions related to a spirit or event.

I have always been intrigued with the mysteries of life and death. However, it wasn't until I moved to Florida that I jumped into the depths of its historic past and started questioning life after death. My interest in the paranormal led me to read several books on the subject... and eventually have my own paranormal experiences. I first set out to investigate one of America's oldest and most haunted towns — St. Augustine, Florida.

I started out by going on several ghost tours in St. Augustine and talking to locals about their paranormal experiences. I then stayed at some of the most haunted inns in the city. I didn't know what to expect, but, to my amazement, I had spirits communicate with me through my dreams and thoughts. I witnessed things move (by spirits) and even saw a full-body apparition!

With each inn I visited, I had more questions. I also had a desire to write about my experiences. I learned that I was a psychic empath...I was able to feel the emotions of spirits and see historic visions of the inn where I was staying. One spirit, named Lavender, from the Kenwood Inn in St. Augustine, reached out to me in a dream and gave me a sign to write a book. She wanted to share her story and, in doing so, led me on a path to write about my experiences and other contact with the spirit world.

I set out on a two-year journey, which took me around the state to discover Florida's "haunted hospitality." While staying in every inn featured in this book, I have experienced paranormal occurrences that I never knew were possible. I have included my experiences along with countless reports from innkeepers, guests, and paranormal experts.

I personally believe that we currently live in a time where there is a thin veil between the living and the dead. A parallel dimension exists for the spirits that have remained here on earth with unfinished business or unresolved issues. Immerse yourself in Florida's haunted hospitality and learn about its history and spirits. Maybe you will be one of the many who will have contact with the *other side*.

Chapter One
Northwest Florida

Monticello ~ Quincy ~ Apalachicola ~ Cedar Key

Monticello

The first Europeans came to Jefferson County in 1528. In the seventeenth century, the Franciscans founded five missions around U.S. Highway 27. Between the eighteenth and nineteenth centuries, the missions were destroyed and the Miccosukee Indians inhabited the area.

In the early 1800s, settlers came to Monticello to plant cotton. The county, named for Thomas Jefferson's Virginia home by the same name, was established on January 6, 1827, and was soon known for producing eighty percent of the world's supply of watermelon seed. Pecans and lumber were also big cash crops for the area.

The city is known for its courthouse, which was dedicated in 1910. The building was designed after the style of Thomas Jefferson's Monticello home. The building housed courts and all county offices, including school administration.

Paranormal Investigators

Big Bend Ghost Trackers
FOUNDER: Betty Davis
PHONE: 850-508-8109
WEBSITE: www.bigbendghosttrackers.com

Betty Davis founded Big Bend Ghost Trackers (BBGT) in 2000. As North Florida's first professional ghost team, their main goal is to "provide service to the living and dead." Betty, a social worker by day, provides paranormal investigations, historical ghost tours, and offers workshops on the paranormal with BBGT. She wants to enlighten and entertain people with the idea that "death is not the end."

Big Bend Ghost Trackers is a nonprofit group of paranormal investigators who use the latest scientific technology, historical evidence, and psychic investigators to provide a service to businesses and homes that may have paranormal activity. They hope to shed light into the situation and resolve any issues that may be occurring. BBGT has investigated several historic inns in North Florida. With their scientific instruments and protocols, they can authenticate a site to be certified haunted using their criteria. As detailed in this book, the Allison Inn in Quincy, the 1872 John Denham House in Monticello, and the Coombs Inn in Apalachicola have all been certified as haunted. BBGT has also held events, including ghost hunting and psychic development seminars, on the weekends at Coombs Inn and the 1872 John Denham House to teach people about the tools and the trade of ghost hunting.

In addition to performing active investigations and giving seminars, Big Bend Ghost Trackers started the Historic Monticello Ghost Tour in 2001. Tours run the last Saturday of the month, and on Fridays and Saturdays of the last two weeks of October. The tour includes fourteen haunted sites that the BBGT has investigated and found to have paranormal activity. This ninety-minute walking tour will take you through Monticello's intriguing history, entertain you with haunted folklore, and provide you with the opportunity to capture paranormal activity for yourself.

The Historic Monticello Ghost Tour begins at the Monticello Chamber of Commerce, 420 Washington Street. You will learn of this building's haunted activity and then be taken across the street to the now vacant 1852 Jefferson County High School. This building was the first brick schoolhouse in Florida, and is now being restored. During restoration, workers have reported hearing children laughing when no one else is around. The next stop on the tour is the 1872 John Denham House. Orbs are frequently captured around the grounds of the inn, so be sure to take your digital camera (and extra batteries) with you.

The highlight of the tour is the Palmer House, which is considered "the most haunted house in the South's most haunted small town." You will be told the story of Dr. John Palmer and his 666 elixir, and how bloodstains keep reappearing on the fireplace. Numerous paranormal reports have been reported about this house over the years.

Other stops on the tour include the hanging tree that is conveniently located in front of Monticello's Historic Courthouse — the spirit of a Civil War soldier has frequently been seen here. Next to the hanging tree stands the Monticello Opera House, another certified haunted location on the tour. The 1890 Monticello Opera House was built by John Perkins, who loved the place so much that his spirit has chosen to remain in the theater after his death in 1927. His presence has been felt and orbs have been captured on the stage.

Several businesses along North Jefferson Street have haunting stories that tour guides will relay to you as you walk along the dark and eerie street. As you walk down North Jefferson Street, you will be taken to the Wirick-Simmins House. This 1831 home is one of the oldest houses in Monticello. Tour guests have photographed apparitions of a woman in pink looking out of the upstairs window and another woman sitting on the porch.

This orb was captured above the Old Jefferson County jail.

To conclude the tour, you may experience the eerie and cold drafts of Dogwood Street while you walk to the old Jefferson County Jail. Some say that ley lines that hold electromagnetic energy are beneath Dogwood Street and attract paranormal energy to the area. Once you get to the jail, you may hear moaning or cell doors rattling from the women's building, even though no prisoners have been housed there for fifty years. The old jail is a perfect place to catch orbs.

For an additional cost, BBGT also offers a 75-minute tour and mini-paranormal investigation of Roseland Cemetery. They will show you how to use several pieces of ghost hunting equipment while you explore some of the oldest graves in Monticello.

If you truly want to immerse yourself into the paranormal, BBGT also offers several ghost hunting and psychic development seminars per year that take place over the course of a weekend. This three-day event provides you with the opportunity to stay at a certified haunted inn and meet with the professional investigators of BBGT. They will teach you about spirits and give you techniques for communicating and capturing scientific evidence of the paranormal. For the latest schedule of events, go to www.bigbendghosttrackers.com.

Monticello's Haunted Sites

Monticello Opera House

This 1890 brick building was built by John H. Perkins. Many think that his spirit still lingers. A dark shadowy man has been seen in the building. People have reported hearing voices, a piano that plays by itself, and the sound of footsteps when no one else is around. Many orbs have been caught in the theater.

Palmer House

This house was originally owned by Dr. John Palmer. It has been a private residence and an antique store. Several different owners have come and gone over the years due to the odd occurrences there. People hear voices and footsteps when no one is around. Bloodstains mysteriously reappear above the fireplace after constantly being painted over and orbs have been caught on camera.

Jefferson County Jail

This early 1900s jail housed both male and female prisoners. Sounds of moaning and cell doors rattling have been heard and orbs have been captured.

Roseland Cemetery

Established in 1827, such prominent locals as the Clarke family and the Denham family are buried at Roseland Cemetery. A high number of Civil War soldiers and infants are also buried here. Due to the yellow fever and influenza epidemics that plagued Monticello in the 1800s, many people died, including many children.

The Big Bend Ghost Trackers offers a paranormal investigation tour of Roseland Cemetery, during which people have caught an apparition of a well-dressed man in a grey suit and top hat. On one occasion, a tour guest disrespected this spirit and was scratched. Strange lights and orbs are often seen and caught on camera.

The Roseland Cemetery is the most haunted cemetery that I have been to. I visited the cemetery on a harvest moon, equipped with my electromagnetic field (EMF) reader and digital camera. On the north end of the cemetery, near the fence, I received high EMF readings. I sensed a spirit presence that continued to follow me throughout the cemetery. I caught an astounding amount of orbs in motion on gravestones. What I didn't expect was that a particular spirit would take interest in me. This spirit decided to follow me back to the bed and breakfast I was staying in, eventually following me home.

What I learned from investigating cemeteries and other haunted locations is that you have to constantly protect yourself at all times. I learned the hard way when I let my guard down at this cemetery. From now on, I protect myself with a vision of white light. I carry sage with me and burn it in my car after I leave a haunted location.

1872 John Denham House

ADDRESS: 555 West Palmer Mill Road
Monticello, FL 32344
PHONE: 850-997-4568
WEBSITE: www.johndenhamhouse.com

The house was built in 1872 by Scottish immigrant John Denham, who dealt in, and prospered on, the cotton trading and shipping businesses. The house has thirteen rooms and is on the National Historic Register. Current owner Pat Inmon has owned the inn since 1997.

Pat had been looking for the perfect inn to buy since 1995. It took her two years to find the 1872 John Denham House. Maybe it was fate that told her to pull off the highway after work one day, as she took the Monticello exit with a "gut feeling." Something led her down West Palmer Mill Road to an overgrown yard, pigeons, and a weathered "For Sale" sign. She knew "this was the house for her." Pat called the realtor and told her that she would buy it.

Pat experiences odd occurrences from day to day. The strangest occurrence has to be the alarm clocks all going off at the same time throughout the house, she says. Pat has no explanation for this, but considers it a reminder that someone else is in the house with her. When Pat first bought the 1872 John Denham house, she opened the sliding wood doors to the parlor that had been closed off for years. When she did, she began hearing old-time music coming from the parlor. Maybe the music was residual energy left from a party held in the parlor a long time ago.

Paranormal occurrences constantly happen in the 1872 John Denham house. Activity has occurred during the day as well as night and has been experienced by guests throughout the house and around the property. Many guests have caught orbs on their cameras both inside and outside of the house. On one of the Historic Monticello Ghost Tours, a person captured a digital picture of an apparition of a lady in white, dressed as a bride in the front yard. Other reports include draining of electronic devices, lights going on and off, and footsteps heard at night when no one is up. Pat herself has heard heavy phantom footsteps at night when no one else is in the house.

The most paranormal activity comes from the Blue Room on the second floor. Aunt Sarah is said to have lived and died in that room. She never married, which may have left her longing for a family in the afterlife. Paranormal activity is heightened when couples with babies or women of child-bearing age stay in the inn. One such couple staying in the Blue Room was awakened in the middle of the night by the light coming on by itself. Several orbs have been captured on camera in the room. Aunt Sarah also makes her presence known with a moral judgment on some guests who have children out of wedlock or non-traditional partners. They are said to get a strong feeling…like they shouldn't be in the house.

I didn't get a chance to stay overnight in the 1872 John Denham House, due to full occupancy when I was there in September 2010; however, I was able to visit the house and spend a couple hours in the afternoon talking with Pat about the paranormal activity at the inn. The minute I walked in the door I felt the paranormal energy in the house. Sitting in the downstairs hallway preparing for my interview, I felt a cold draft come over me and sensed something was there watching me. I decided to walk around the inside of the house to see if I was able to pick up on more paranormal energy. On my way upstairs to the cupola to take pictures, I noticed my camera batteries were almost completely drained. This phenomenon follows the reports of guests' electronic devices being drained. Other reports include people sensing the spirit of the original owner, John Denham, in the cupola. Betty Davis, founder of BBGT, believes John Denham's spirit still watches the neighborhood from his unique watchtower.

Pat believes there is a feeling of protection over the house and guests. In the Green Room on the second floor, a spirit is said to make guests feel comfortable. One couple who stayed in the Green Room reported the room nice and cold when they checked in. It was odd since most of the house was set at a warmer temperature. Years ago, Pat's daughter, who was pregnant with twins, stayed in the Green Room. A picture of her daughter was taken in the room and several orbs were captured around her. Pat felt the orbs were a foreshadowing of events that were to come.

However, one of the inn's spirits appears to look out for Pat's well-being. When Pat is on the second story doing housework, she will throw towels down the stairs over the railing. One time she may have leaned over the railing too far and an unseen force pushed her back to safety. Another time, Pat was lighting the fire in the fireplace just a little too close and something pushed her back.

In 2003, *USA Today* declared the 1872 John Denham House the second most haunted inn in the United States — and a place to go to sleep with a ghost. I definitely felt paranormal energy the minute I walked into the house. The spirits that reside here had loved the house so much when they were alive they decided to stay in the afterlife. Whether they make their presence known through their energy, orbs, or protection, they make the 1872 John Denham House a perfect example of haunted hospitality.

J.M. Henry House
ADDRESS: 525 East High Street
Monticello, FL 32344
PHONE: 850-933-0456
WEBSITE: www.jmhenry.com

This house was built in 1884 by John M. Henry, who established the Monticello Power Company, operated a lumber mill, and was a member of the city council for eighteen years. The home remained in the Henry family for five generations. Originally, the left side of the house was a large dining room and hosted dances in the late 1800s. The house was later split into three apartments; the granddaughter-in-law lived in the lower left wing and managed the house until 2007. According to family history, throughout the years several children were born in the house. At one point, a fire destroyed the house's original lattice work.

Pat Inmon, owner of the 1872 John Denham House, also restored the J.M. Henry in 2008, with current owner Jerry Frederick. She rents out the J.M. Henry House as a vacation rental and rents out rooms when the 1872 John Denham House is full.

The J.M. Henry House has had paranormal activity, according to Big Bend Ghost Trackers. The paranormal investigating group has taken people on a tour of the house only to have them hear voices in the parlor when no one was staying in the house. BBGT team member Lisa personally saw an apparition of a woman in period dress sitting in a chair next to the second floor staircase. Another team member witnessed lights flicker on and off in the downstairs bathroom when no one was around.

I had the chance to stay the night in the house alone. I had chosen the downstairs Blue Room at first, but I then got an unusual feeling that I shouldn't stay in this particular room, which was possibly the area that the granddaughter of the family lived in. I listened to my intuition and moved upstairs to the Peach Room. Unfortunately, nothing paranormal occurred the night I stayed there, but a colleague of mine, Psychic Medium Gemini Rose, saw a picture of the J.M. Henry House that I had taken and remarked that a lot of residual energy still lingers inside.

If you get a chance to stay in the J.M. Henry House, you will get to stay in a beautifully restored and historic house. The atmosphere is peaceful and sophisticated. Although the paranormal activity is sporadic, you can almost imagine the house alive with social activities during the 1800s.

Avera-Clarke House Bed & Breakfast

ADDRESS: 580 West Washington Street
P.O. Box 980
Monticello, FL 32344
PHONE: 850-997-5007
WEBSITE: www.averaclarke.com

The Avera-Clarke House was built in 1890 by Judge Thomas Clarke, a Confederate Civil War veteran. He practiced law and founded the Farmers and Merchants Bank in 1906. In 1885, he became the mayor of Monticello. He and his wife, Daisy Bird Clarke, had four children: Scott Dilworth, Kate, John Weldon, and William Clarke. Thomas Clarke died in 1900 of apoplexy. It was a shock to the entire community, for he was a well-respected judge and character. His wake was held inside the house. His son, S. D. Clarke, also became a judge and politician. S. D. Clarke was the last Clarke to occupy the house.

Gretchen and Troy Avera bought the house in 2002 and opened it as a bed and breakfast in 2003. They also saved a historic cottage from the 1820s that was said to be the oldest structure in Jefferson County from being torn down in 2006. Gretchen had an inclination to track down the property manager and said everything she could to prevent the house from being demolished. One week later, the manager offered the cottage to Gretchen. Soon Gretchen and Troy moved the 900-square-foot cottage, located one block southeast of the courthouse, to the Avera-Clarke House property. The cottage is fully restored and used for special events.

Gretchen and Troy were only visiting Monticello when Gretchen fell in love with the Clarke House that was for sale. Within minutes, the couple called the realtor. It didn't take long for them to sell their own house and move in. Upon doing so, Gretchen decorated the house with her own eclectic style. Art deco artwork, angels, and huntery decorate the house and cottage.

Gretchen doesn't personally "connect with anything paranormal in the house." However, she does recall "the oddest thing happening" when she first moved in. While arranging the furniture, she had placed a glass shelf cabinet in front of the dining room fireplace. No sooner than she had, the glass shelves inside the case shattered for no apparent reason.

The dining room fireplace is known to be surrounded by spiritual energy. Big Bend Ghost Trackers visited the Avera-Clarke House and took a picture of an orb above the fireplace. Several years later, Scott Dilworth, son of Thomas Clarke, visited the house and recalled seeing his father's casket lay in front of the dining room fireplace during his wake, so perhaps this location harbors some residual energy left behind from years past.

Judge Thomas Clarke's spirit may still be around, looking after his house and the townspeople that he spent so much time thinking about. Gretchen believes the back of the house, where their living quarters are, is where Thomas Clarke's bedroom used to be. A few times the Averas' dogs have been startled in the middle of the night by something. They start to bark or become anxious.

Thomas Clarke's spirit may have shown himself to particular guests who stay in the house, especially attorneys who come to the area for court. One time an attorney was staying in the Queen Anne Room, only to be awakened in the middle of the night. He said that a person came to him while he was laying in bed and stood there and looked at him. Being very logical, he thought it was a dream. He soon realized it wasn't a dream, but a peaceful and unexplained experience. Could this have been the spirit of Thomas Clarke looking over his house and reaching out to a fellow attorney?

I had the chance to stay in the French Country Room for two nights. The first night I slept very peacefully. The second night I felt a lot of energy in the air due to the full harvest moon. I went to bed around midnight only to be awakened at 3 a.m. to an unknown energy. I almost sensed that someone was caressing my arm. After that, it took me a while to go back to sleep. When I shared my experience with Gretchen in the morning, she said that several of her dogs became anxious about something around 3 in the morning also. Could this have been a spirit's way of trying to get my attention to tell me something?

The Avera-Clarke House has had paranormal activity inside the house as well as outside the property. One evening, while on the second floor, I was able to capture a series of orbs at the base of the stairway. I took another series of photos of the grounds surrounding the historic cottage. I also caught an orb in front of the cottage. One guest even reported seeing an apparition of a woman sitting on the porch of the cottage.

Orbs captured at the bottom of a stairway at the Avera-Clarke House.

I definitely felt energy from the cottage's historic past. It is said that a single woman from the 1800s once owned the cottage and raised a few children on her own there. I could feel the spirit's hardship and attachment to the cottage. I feel that the spirit longed for an easier life, maybe even a man to take care of her. Her feelings may still linger for a happier life. The cottage is now rented out for special events such as weddings, which may be a little hard for the spirit to bear.

In all my experiences of staying in Florida's haunted inns, I never thought that my work with the paranormal would follow me home. It wasn't until I stayed at the Avera-Clarke House that I opened my eyes wider to what was possible in the paranormal realm.

I had received premonitions about my trip to Monticello when I left my house in Daytona Beach. I started to have psychic visions of my car breaking down. When I first arrived at the Avera-Clarke House, my car was making weird noises and I had to take it to a mechanic in town. I was only supposed to stay one night at the inn, but due to my car problems, I had to stay another night.

It was on the second night that fate — and unexplained paranormal activity — attached itself to me. Since I was in town an extra day, I decided to visit the Roseland Cemetery on the harvest moon. I had my EMF reader with me that night and I experienced a continual energy that followed me throughout the cemetery. I was able to catch so many orbs in motion that I couldn't believe my eyes. I didn't think that a spirit might follow me back to the inn, but that night…I felt something touch my arm and wake me from my sleep. I didn't think anything of it until I tried to leave Monticello the following morning.

After checking out of the Avera-Clarke House, several odd things started happening to me. Upon leaving Monticello, my car broke down at a gas station by Interstate 10. The mechanics who worked on my car that week picked me up and couldn't explain how the car part had loosened and poured gas all over. When I finally got my car fixed again, I continued my drive home. I felt as though something was with me in the car. I was overwhelmed by a sick, sinking feeling in my stomach all the way home to Daytona Beach.

When I finally arrived home, I couldn't eat, sleep, or think clearly for a week. I had to know what was going on, so I consulted with Psychic Medium Gemini Rose about my experience in Monticello. She said that a woman spirit could relate to me. She had attached herself to me to tell her story. Since I was feeling overwhelmed by the spirit's presence, Gemini told me to sage my house. She also told the spirit to back off a bit. After that, I felt a little better, but continued to have strange dreams. In those dreams, I was told pieces of this spirit's life story. I was told the spirit's full name, birth and death dates, how she died, and a vision of what she looked like when she was alive. I was told by the spirit to go back to Monticello and to research her story.

When I went to Monticello, I talked to Gretchen and told her what had happened to me. I asked Gretchen about the spirit and if she had any links to the cottage. The spirit might have lived in the cottage at one time. I then went to the Thomasville Historical Library and found a record of the spirit's name and the dates that she lived in Monticello. I even found her family's plots at the Roseland Cemetery. I was able to leave the spirit behind in Monticello. Her memory is still with me, as I promised to one day discover and write her story.

My experience in Monticello on the harvest moon left me pondering the extent to which spirits will go to communicate with us. While my experience at the Avera-Clarke House has seemed to be extraordinary, the overall vibration of the house is peaceful and comforting. Gretchen and Troy don't advertise the house as paranormal, although there have been a few unexplained things that have occurred — and it is possible that one of the spirits might reach out and make themselves known to the right person.

Quincy

In 1821, John Wood from New York came to Quincy to settle the land from a friend's granted claim. Others followed suit and the area was known as the Bluffs. It wasn't until 1825 that the county was named "Quincy" after the president, John Quincy Adams. The public square was also called "John's Square" after the president.

Quincy was incorporated as a town in 1834 and as a city in 1840. Flour and saw mills flourished. Skilled German immigrants and craftsmen settled there, and Quincy became an important place to conduct business and politics. In 1858, the famous Lincoln-Douglas debates were held in Washington Park, or John's Square, to discuss the issue of slavery within the states. Slavery was a hot topic in Quincy. Most citizens were abolitionists and played an important part in the Underground Railroad.

Quincy's Haunted Sites

Allison House Inn
ADDRESS: 215 North Madison Street
Quincy, FL 32351
PHONE: 888-904-2511
WEBSITE: www.allisonhouseinn.com

The Allison House Inn was built in 1843 by A.K. Allison, who was a general commanding the wars resulting from the Indian Removal Act in the 1830s. Allison moved to Quincy in 1843 and built the original house on King and Madison streets. He was Speaker of the Florida House in 1852, president of the Florida Senate, and governor of the state of Florida in 1865. In office, he signed a peace treaty with the union ending Florida's role in the Civil War. He was the only person to occupy the three highest offices in the Florida state government.

In 1867, Allison married his second wife, Elizabeth Susan Coleman, and they had a daughter named Sarah, who was born in the house. Allison died in 1893 and his wife died two years later. Sarah inherited the house and moved in with her husband Ross Gilliam Harris. In 1925, Sarah raised the house up on brick pilings to create the two-story house of today. She operated the second level as a boarding house while living in the downstairs apartment. Sarah died in the 1940s. After that, a new owner rented out two apartments upstairs and ran a credit bureau downstairs. In 1990, the house was converted into Quincy's first bed and breakfast.

Stuart and Eileen Johnson first saw the house/inn in 1995 and purchased it in 1996 after an extensive search for the perfect inn.

Stuart said he had never experienced anything paranormal in the house; in fact, the house remained pretty quiet until his sister-in-law came to visit and stayed in the Garden Room. She claims to have awakened in the middle of the night to see an apparition of a woman dressed in white sitting in the chair across the room. On a different occasion, the sister-in-law attempted to sleep in the Garden Room again. She got up in the middle of the night to turn down the temperature and noticed the same woman in white sitting on the end of the bed.

In 2002, Stuart and Eileen were in Monticello taking a tour of historic homes when they met members of the Big Bend Ghost Trackers. Eileen told them the story of her sister seeing an apparition of a ghost and invited the team to come to the Allison House to do an investigation.

BBGT went to the Allison House to do an investigation in June of that year. Members stayed the night in both the Governor's Room and the Garden Room. The Governor's Room was the parlor of the original one-story house while the Garden Room was Sarah Allison's childhood room.

During the investigation, members of BBGT sensed that there were four spirits in the house: two gentlemen named Greenfield and Anderson, A.K. Allison, and Allison's daughter Sarah. A.K. Allison was sensed walking down the hallway at night by the investigators while Sarah was seen and felt by them in her childhood room, the Garden Room.

While conducting historical research on the two gentlemen, they found that there was an extended family member named "Granville" and five families in the area named Anderson.

When BBGT investigated the Garden Room, two members made contact with the spirit of Sarah. Later, around 2:25 in the morning, a temperature change was recorded by the night stand with their digital thermometer. They also got a spike in the EMF detector after the temperature changed. The same electromagnetic force and temperature change occurred in the Governor's Room while members investigated there. In addition to the scientific evidence, as well as various personal experiences, BBGT caught orbs on camera in the upstairs hallway and a ribbon of smoke coming up the stairway on a video recording.

A.K. Allison.

I had the chance to stay in the Garden Room, as I wanted to experience the reports for myself. The first thing I noticed when checking in was how cold the room was. That day was extremely hot, so the drastic cold was quite a shock. Eileen had to adjust the temperature for me. After I settled in, the temperature in the room kept changing drastically by itself. I had to manually move it to 80 degrees to shut it off and then it would get really hot. I then lowered it a few degrees and it would get frigid. I kept changing the thermostat over and over my entire stay. The temperature changes within the room were so drastic that I woke up around 2 in the morning. I was so cold I had to sleep with my bathrobe on. The next morning at breakfast, I asked the couple that was staying in the Governor's Room how they slept. The woman said that she was so cold that she had to sleep with her jacket on. I didn't think much of the temperature change as paranormal until I asked Stuart about the air units. He said that each room has their own separate unit that has to be manually adjusted.

Along with the temperature changes, I also got energy spikes on my EMF detector while staying in the Garden Room. I had done several EMF readings around the room to check for energy. The EMF readings for the room were normal until I started reading various ghost and history books while in bed. I got a strange feeling on the bed next to me, so I decided to do an EMF reading. I was a little surprised when the EMF meter spiked to "orange" for high electromagnetic energy…It felt like someone was sitting next to me in bed.

I began to sense that a spirit was next to me, interested in what I was doing. I then tried to communicate with the spirit by placing the meter over the books. It lit up "red," indicating high energy for the ghost books, and went back to normal for the history books. I then found a picture in the history book of A.K. Allison and asked the spirit to light up the meter if I was communicating with Allison. It didn't light up, so I felt like I was communicating with Sarah. I felt like she was making her presence known and helping me with my writing. I wanted to be sure about the authenticity of the EMF readings, so I continued to check around the bed and electrical outlets for energy spikes. I found the energy was coming from the top of the bed. I couldn't explain the steady hit being so far away from a power source.

While reflecting on my experience, I feel I had similar experiences of temperature changes and EMF readings compared to what BBGT's evidence showed of the Allison House Inn. I feel that we both made spiritual contact with Sarah and that her presence can still be felt in the room and house she loved so much.

There are several books to read at the inn on the history of Quincy, in addition to the book of evidence from BBGT certifying the Allison House Inn as being officially haunted.

Quincy Leaf Theater

Built in the 1940s, it was the premier movie theater up until the 1960s. In 1983, while performing shows there, the Quincy music group witnessed many paranormal occurrences. Doors slamming shut by themselves, objects moving of their own volition, and apparitions of a man in a derby hat and a young girl were seen in the auditorium.

Employees have said that they felt like they were being watched, and they have also experienced extreme cold spots.

Garden Room bed.

Apalachicola

Settlers arrived in the 1820s to take advantage of land that was perfect for growing cotton. By 1831, Apalachicola became the third largest cotton port along the Gulf Coast, shipping cotton to Europe and New England. In the 1850s, the railroads were re-routed and Apalachicola's cotton trade dwindled. When the Confederacy embarked on a blockade of Apalachicola's harbor, there was a decline in the economy until the lumber boom of the 1880s. It wasn't until the 1930s that Apalachicola began to capitalize on their natural resources of sponges and seafood.

Apalachicola's Haunted Sites

Orman House

In 1838, the home belonged to Thomas Orman. During the Civil War, Confederate soldiers guarded the house and would warn townspeople of Union soldiers with nail keg on the roof. Apparitions of soldiers have been seen and doors have been known to slam shut by themselves.

Chestnut Cemetery

This cemetery dates back to the earliest days of Apalachicola, when the town was often plagued by death of malaria, yellow fever, ship wrecks, and hurricanes. The oldest tombstone is from 1831, though some unmarked graves from earlier years may still exist.

Many important people in American history are buried here, including the famous botanist Dr. Alvin Wentworth Chapman. He lived in Apalachicola for fifty years and wrote several books on ecology. Union and Confederate soldiers share graves side by side here. With all the disasters and disease that took place on the island, a few wandering spirits may still exist and have even been captured on film.

Orb captured above a gravestone in Chestnut Cemetery.

Coombs House Inn
ADDRESS: 80 Sixth Street
Apalachicola, FL 32320
PHONE: 888-244-8320
WEBSITE: www.coombshouseinn.com

 With the help of local builder George H. Marshall, James N. Coombs built the Coombs House in 1905. Though Marshall built other well-known Victorian houses in Apalachicola in the late 1800s to the early 1900s, at the time, the Coombs' House was Apalachicola's finest home.

James N. Coombs moved to Apalachicola in 1877 with his childhood sweetheart Maria Stareett and was very successful in everything he did. Mr. Coombs established three sawmills, the First National Bank of Apalachicola, and the Coombs Company, which exported pine and cypress lumber to destinations around the world. Mr. Coombs had his house built to reflect his status and success. Unique to the house is the custom-built front door, measuring forty-two inches wide, large enough for a coffin to be placed in the house for a wake. Doors were commonly built this way, for people treasured their homes so much that they wanted to be presented in their homes for viewing upon their deaths.

Death came a little too soon for both Coombs. On March 6, 1911, around 1 a.m., a fire broke out while James and Maria were sleeping. Though they were not injured, flames engulfed the roof. Water from three horse-drawn fire companies and smoke destroyed most of their beloved possessions and left the house in disarray. Heartbroken, the Coombs' moved into the Franklin Hotel. Many people think the couple fell into a state of depression and gave up on the idea of ever returning to their grand home. Maria died March 16, 1911; James died April 8, 1911.

Many townspeople were shocked at the couples' sudden deaths. Bill Spohrer, current owner of the Coombs House Inn and local historian, thinks the Coombs' might have inhaled toxic fumes from the burned lead paint when they were in the house trying to salvage their belongings. The *Apalachicola Times* from April 15, 1911, has an article written about Mr. Coombs' death and funeral. The cause of death was listed as being from an unknown illness.

A funeral for Mr. Coombs was held in the church across the street from his house. The first floor of the house had little fire damage, so Mr. Coombs' body was displayed in the parlor for his wake, which lasted two days. Both Mr. and Mrs. Coombs are buried, side-by-side, in the Chestnut Street Cemetery, just across the street from their beloved house.

The Coombs House was eventually repaired and handed down to family through the years. In the 1960s, the house was boarded up, vandalized, and left vacant…until Lynn Wilson and Bill Spohrer had a calling to visit Apalachicola. While living in Miami, the couple saw an ad in the *Miami Herald* about visiting Apalachicola. They called the number in the ad…only to be surprised that the realtor was Bill Spohrer's unknown second cousin. As fate would have it, the couple took a trip to Apalachicola and fell in love with the history of the town as well as the rundown Coombs House.

Lynn is an artistic, well-known interior designer and she saw the opportunity to restore and bring renewed life to the deteriorated house. When they saw the Coombs House, it was an "absolute mess," Bill recalled. It took them two years to track down the Coombs' family members to sell them the house. It took another two years to restore the house. They wanted the house to be something the town could be proud of. They painted it bright yellow, much to the town's surprise, and opened it as an inn in August 1994. In 1998, Lynn and Bill purchased the house next-door, which they restored and opened up as the Coombs Villas. In 2007, they purchased the in-law house next door to that and named it the Coombs Veranda Suites.

Over the years, Lynn and Bill have hired several people to manage and run the inn. Most of the paranormal reports come from the employees who have spent most of their time in the house.

One of the most significant reports is from Lynn and Bill's daughter-in-law, Anna Maria, who ran the inn for awhile. Anna was in the kitchen during a hurricane when she saw a man in old-fashioned clothes walk through the dining room. She saw the apparition continue through the foyer and walk right *through* the wall of the first floor guest room. The man she saw is said to resemble Mr. Coombs. His apparition was also seen reflected in the first floor glass door and windows prior to a hurricane. Some say that Mr. Coombs was watching out for his beloved house to prevent another disaster.

I got the chance to spend the night in the Wilson Room. This room used to be the parlor of the original house and is now a guest room. Reading the *Apalachicola Times* of April 15, 1911, I discovered that Mr. Coombs' wake had been held in what is now the Wilson Room. His body was displayed for two days until his funeral. Estella, the current innkeeper, says that several times she will go into the Wilson Room for something and find an indentation on the bed like someone had been lying on it. She will straighten the sheets and it will happen again. There is a possibility that the bed is in the very spot where the coffin lay. The night I stayed in the room, I had a little trouble sleeping. I woke around 3 a.m. and could not go back to sleep. The next morning I read the guest journal from the Wilson Room; in February 2010, a couple reported that they had a good stay there, "but you will wake up at 3:00 a.m. on the dot every night by something."

Other paranormal activity has been reported by employees and guests in rooms 5 and 8 on the second floor; Margaret, the housekeeper, heard children's laughter and playing coming from Room 5. I toured Room 5 upon check-in and took a couple of pictures. Later in the evening I went upstairs to check things out. I found the light on in the bathroom of Room 5 as well as the fan. No guests were staying in the room, and the light and fan were not on in the afternoon. I couldn't quite explain this as paranormal, but thought it was odd.

Room 8 has had a couple of spirit reports from guests. The room used to be Mr. Coombs' bedroom. A couple of guests have felt Mr. Coombs' presence at night, but, for the most part, couples enjoy this room as their honeymoon suite and have nothing but good reports written about their stay in the guest journal. This room was the Coombs' pride and joy.

Wilson Room.

Other strange occurrences have happened around the house for no reason. Destiny is another innkeeper who has experienced a couple of odd occurrences in the house while alone. While working one afternoon, she heard a door banging upstairs. When she went to investigate, the porch door was open and banging from the wind. She couldn't explain it since no guests were in the house. Another odd thing was that one of the guest rooms had been locked by an unseen hand. Estella also witnessed bolts in the front door coming out of the handle for no apparent reason.

Reports are not only tied to the main house, but the Coombs Villas as well. Destiny said that a guest once called her at 2 in the morning from Room 17, complaining about children upstairs playing with a ball. Destiny told the man that there wasn't even an upstairs to the house.

The Big Bend Ghost Trackers investigated the Coombs House Inn in September 2009. They experienced knocks on doors, doors opening and closing by themselves, and unexplained footsteps. While staying in Room 8, they recorded the door opening and a spirit coming in and standing by the end of the bed. They analyzed the evidence they had gathered and certified the Coombs House Inn as "haunted."

Cedar Key

The Cedar Keys were inhabited as early as 500 B.C., and later used by the Seminole Indians, Spanish, and pirates, such as Jean Lafitte and Captain Kidd, as a watering stop for ships returning to Spain from Mexico. In 1842, the United States Congress had enacted the Armed Occupation Act to force the Seminoles from the territory and to stimulate White settlement in Florida.

Cedar Key occupied a critical location during the Civil War. Blockade-runners exported cotton and lumber and imported food and other supplies to the Confederacy. The Union occupied the Cedar Keys in early 1864 and stayed there for the remainder of the war. Repairs to the Florida Railroad were completed in 1868 and freight and passenger traffic again flowed into Cedar Key. The town of Cedar Keys was incorporated in 1869. A hurricane all but destroyed the small town in 1896.

Cedar Key's Haunted Sites

Island Hotel & Restaurant
ADDRESS: 373 2nd Street
P.O. Box 460
Cedar Key, FL 32625
PHONE: 352-543-5111
WEBSITE: www.islandhotel-cedarkey.com

The Island Hotel is listed on the National Register of Historic Places. The building was constructed in 1859 and is built from seashell tabby with oak supports that have withstood the worst hurricanes. The building was originally built as a general store and post office.

Major Parsons built the structure and named it Parson and Hale's General Store. During the Civil War, Union soldiers burned down almost every building in Cedar Key except the general store. They used the hotel as officer quarters and a warehouse. Just before the end of the Civil War, the Confederacy retook the town and officers of the Southern Army were billeted in the hotel.

After the war, the general store was reopened. It also served as a customs house and headquarters for the Cedar Key Post Office. In the 1880s, the building functioned as a restaurant and boardinghouse. In 1896, a major hurricane severely damaged the town and the store. In 1914, Langdon Parsons sold the building to Simon Feinberg, who turned the building into the Bay Hotel.

The Bay Hotel was managed by a man named Markham. It is said that Simon Feinberg found out about an illegal liquor still Markham had built in the attic. Feinberg was against this because of his religious upbringing. He confronted Markham about the still, which led to an altercation. That night Markham died of food poisoning.

Simon Feinberg...he owned the hotel in 1914.

The hotel went through many owners, name changes, and natural disasters. The hotel nearly burned to the ground during the Great Depression when it operated as a speakeasy and brothel. During World War II, the hotel became rundown and was uninhabitable.

In 1946, Bessie and Loyal Gibbs bought the building and restored it, naming it the Island Hotel. During their ownership, the hotel and bar became a notable hangout for local characters and celebrities, including Pearl Buck, Vaughan Monroe, Tennessee Erie Ford, Francis Langford, Myrna Loy, Richard Boone, and John MacDonald. Jimmy Buffet even played at the Neptune Lounge during the 1980s. In the 1950s, a hurricane took the roof off the hotel. Major remodeling was required to make the building usable again. Loyal Gibbs died in 1962, but Bessie continued to operate the Island Hotel until her own health began to decline in 1973.

Andy Bair has owned the Island Hotel for six and a half years. He was just passing through Cedar Key when he found a real estate agent who showed him the hotel. Says Bair, "It was a fit from the time I walked in." At first, he was "not a firm believer in the paranormal," but there were too many things going on for him not to believe. One of his most memorable experiences included smelling a phantom wet dog that came and went.

The rooms with the most paranormal reports are 27, 28, and 29. In rooms 27 and 28, it is rumored that the spirit of a murdered prostitute lingers. It is said that while guests are asleep the spirit kisses them on the cheek and disappears. Andy recalls that six months after he purchased the hotel, his daughter-in-law was staying in Room 27 with her cat. While they were sleeping, the cat "got spooked" and she woke up to see an apparition of a man with bushy gray hair and a mustache disappear through the wall. This man is said to resemble one of the prior owners, Simon Feinberg. A picture of him can be seen at the end of the hallway on the second floor. Housekeepers also report seeing wet footprints on the floors and body imprints on quilts and pillows even when no guests are staying in the hotel.

The most talked about ghost of the Island Hotel is the previous owner, Bessie Gibbs. She was such a character in life that it would only seem right that her spirit carries on for her in the afterlife. As Cedar Key's mayor, Bessie achieved a lot with the town and the hotel. Guests staying in her old room, #29, most often report a presence.

Room 29…Bessie Gibbs' original room.

In some extreme cases, they are locked out of the room. Bessie is also reported to move furniture, pictures, and close doors. Some people have smelled cigar smoke in her room even though no smoking is allowed in the hotel. You are reminded that the room used to be Bessie's when you see the custom letter "G" on the cupboard knobs in the bathroom.

I had the chance to stay in Room 29. Upon arriving at the hotel, I came to find out that I was the only guest registered. I was a little apprehensive about staying the night alone in such a big hotel and joked about it with the clerk, Rhonda, at the front desk. When I went up to Room 29 to unlock the door, the door opened all by itself…Maybe I was being welcomed by Bessie.

Andy says that every couple of months some sort of paranormal activity is reported throughout the hotel. Simon Feinberg is said to be a wandering spirit, possibly keeping watch on the hotel in the afterlife. Molly Brown, who worked at the hotel for more than twenty years, saw a figure in the lobby that just evaporated away. One paranormal group that stayed at the Island Hotel caught evidence of a shadow walking across the upstairs porch. This might have been the southern army soldier who has been seen by several guests through the years. He is said to stand guard on the second floor near the double doors to the balcony.

The other tragic spirit that haunts the Island Hotel is a nine-year-old black boy who possibly drowned in the basement's cistern. He was thought to have worked at the hotel when it was a general store. He was accused of stealing and had gone to the cistern to hide. It is thought that he eventually drowned. Jan, the chef of the hotel, even saw the apparition of the little boy raiding the pantry closet.

Many characters have lived in and visited the Island Hotel throughout the years. One of the highlights of the hotel is the Neptune Bar and Lounge. It has a lovely mural painted behind the bar. If you look closely at the 1940s mural of King Neptune, you might notice several bullet holes in it. Andy says that a rowdy fisherman fired them back in the day, protecting his wife from the wandering eyes of Shorty, the bartender. If you get a chance to meet Andy, some say that he is the spitting image of King Neptune in the mural.

The Island Hotel will take you back in history. You will get a feeling of the island and its relaxed atmosphere while staying here. You might also pick up on the energy that was left behind from previous guests and owners. The people who owned the building had strong personalities and may have left their energy and presence behind.

Shell Mound

The shell mound is thousands of years old and consists of a .3 mile trail to the mound, which is surrounded by a wildlife estuary. Pirates are said to have hid their treasure on the mound and were caught by a girl named Annie and her dog, both of whom were killed and buried on the mound. Many people, including Annie's father, have seen her spirit while fishing. People have also seen a white light chasing "Annie and her dog."

Cedar Key Cemetery

The cemetery is located on the historic island of Atsena Otie Key. The island was home to the original town built in the Cedar Keys that consisted of several hundred residents. The Eberhard Faber Pencil Company also had a factory on the island in the 1890s. The town was all but wiped out when the hurricane of 1896 hit the island.

Today, the island of Atsena Otie Key is managed by the Cedar Keys National Wildlife Refuge and has a nice boardwalk around the cemetery. There is an abandoned anchor, and the remnants of the old main street is now a path through the woods under a canopy of oak trees.

This is a unique cemetery that holds a lot of history while overlooking a beautiful preserve. However, like most cemeteries, it is a little eerie at night, though it is also a good place to take pictures.

Chapter Two
Northeast Florida

High Springs ~ Gainesville ~ Micanopy ~ St. Augustine ~ Amelia Island

High Springs

Hernando de Soto led his expedition through this area around 1539. In the seventeenth century, Indian villages and a large Spanish mission flourished near the Ichetucknee and Santa Fe rivers.

The northwest region of Alachua County was first settled in the 1830s, but it wasn't until 1884 that High Springs began to flourish as a result of the Western Railroad that extended from Live Oak to Gainesville. In the next few years, High Springs boomed from the development of phosphate mining in the area. In 1892, the town was incorporated and became an important railroad center. In later years, High Springs became the antique capital of North Central Florida.

High Springs' Haunted Sites

Grady House

ADDRESS: 420 NW 1st Avenue
High Springs, FL 32655
PHONE: 386-454-2206
WEBSITE: www.gradyhouse.com

Around the turn of the century, the Grady House was the town's first bakery named Nisi. In 1917, a second story was added and it became a boardinghouse for railroad workers and supervisors. The house was owned by H. McL. Grady, who was the mayor of High Springs at the time. In the 1960s it was rented out as apartments and fell into a state of disrepair. In the 1990s, a couple bought the house and turned it into an inn.

Paul and Lucie Regensdorf were looking to buy an inn in the southeast over four years ago and decided to look at property in Florida. They had never been to High Springs before and fell in love with the house when an inn broker showed it to them. They have owned the Grady House since August 2006.

Lucie has always believed in the paranormal. She has had paranormal experiences in a previous house they owned in New York. Lucie believes that there is something in the Grady House that she can't quite explain, as she has "felt a presence" around her when no one else is around. While sleeping one night in their apartment at the back of the house, she heard a male voice that her dog growled at. She didn't feel like checking it out so she went back to sleep. She often feels like she sees something like a shadow around the house, but it is "never frightening." She believes whoever it is likes to "take care of the house."

One such spirit likes to tidy things up and make sure guests are comfortable in their rooms. In the Red Room, an apparition of a woman has been seen in the mirror. Guests have reported someone tucking them into bed at night in the Red, Peach, and Yellow rooms. Lucie told me a story of a female guest that was staying in the Peach Room. She had been reading magazines on her bed one evening and left the books sprawled out on top of the sheets when she went to sleep. When she awoke, the magazines were in a straight pile on the bedside table. Another time, a gentleman guest staying in the Peach Room got really upset because he said that someone sat on the edge of the bed and smoothed out the sheets beside him.

I had the chance to stay in the warm and cozy Peach Room. While I didn't experience anything significantly paranormal that night, I did wake up to find the comforter pleated three times. I found that odd since I usually toss and turn at night, disrupting the sheets completely.

In addition to the Grady House, Lucie also rents out the Skeet Cottage that is next door. The cottage is a two-story Victorian home built in 1896. Wanetta Skeet was the prior owner; she died in the house in 1997. Wanetta was the first female mayor of High Springs and owned a local service station and restaurant. Strange things have been reported there, says Lucie. The swing sways by itself and stomping has been heard upstairs when no one is in the house.

The Grady House is a perfect example of haunted hospitality. From being an original bakery to a boardinghouse and bed and breakfast, the spirits and energy here want to make your stay as comfortable as possible.

Micanopy

The land first belonged to the Potanos people. Hernando de Soto explored the land in 1539, and later the Spanish brought warfare and disease to the area and its inhabitants. The Seminoles later occupied the territory in the 1700s.

The town of Micanopy was founded in 1821 by Edward Wanton and Moses Levy. Fort Defiance was built in the 1830s to protect Micanopy's settlers from Seminole Indian raids. The fort was evacuated and burned in 1836, closed in 1843, and reopened off and on until 1856. Today, Micanopy's historic district encompasses thirty-eight buildings that are on the National Register of Historic Places.

Micanopy's Haunted Sites

Herlong Mansion
ADDRESS: 402 NE Cholokka Boulevard
P.O. Box 667
Micanopy, Florida 32667
PHONE: 352-466-3322
WEBSITE: www.herlong.com

This 1845 pine farm home belonged to the Simonton family, the original settlers of Micanopy. Natalie Simonton inherited the house around the turn of the century and moved to Micanopy with her husband, Zeddy Clarence ("ZC") Herlong, a prosperous lumber and citrus entrepreneur. They remodeled the house in 1909, transforming it into the Greek Revival style that the mansion is today.

ZC and Natalie raised six children for whom the mansion rooms are named. When Natalie passed away in 1950, she left the Herlong Mansion to her six children equally, with the understanding that their father could live there until his death. ZC died ten years later; after he passed, the six siblings fought for eighteen years over ownership of the house.

Inez Herlong Miller moved into the house when she had accumulated enough money to buy out her siblings' share of the house. Inez lived on the first floor and died at age sixty-eight in a hospital. Inez's son inherited the house, but was unable to keep up with the property. In 1986, the mansion was purchased by a couple from Orlando. Soon after, in the 1990s, it was sold to Sonny Howard, who restored and converted the mansion into a bed and breakfast. Sonny took the open attic space on the third floor and converted it into additional guest rooms that resemble the rest of the house. Current owner Carolyn West purchased the Herlong Mansion in December 2005.

Before coming to Micanopy, Carolyn owned another famous haunted inn in Key West named the Eaton Lodge, where she had her first memorable paranormal experience. Carolyn and her husband lived in Key West for eleven years before a buyer made them an offer on the Eaton Lodge; they then set out to find another inn. When her husband saw the Herlong Mansion for sale, he fell in love with it and everything else fell into place. Although Carolyn doesn't openly promote the ghost legends of the mansion to guests, she personally "believes in the spiritual world."

Carolyn says that the ghostly legends were accumulated by the previous owner, Sonny Howard, to stir interest in the inn. Sonny claimed that former owner, Inez Herlong Miller, died in her childhood room and haunts the inn. There are no records of Inez dying in the house. Carolyn says that Sonny had built the additional rooms on the third floor and claimed it was Inez's room to draw in guests. During that time, all the guest rooms were named after the six Herlong children. Carolyn renamed the rooms when she bought the inn to change the reputation of the inn as being haunted.

When Carolyn first opened the inn, she says she experienced a lot of difficult and strange occurrences. She claims that she went through several "tests" by an unseen force that she had to overcome. Plumbing pipes came crashing down and the sewer started to act up within the first week. Another day, a returning guest staying in the Jasmine Room leaned up against a tiled shower wall and fell through to the attic. Carolyn believes that she went through these "trials," possibly overseen by the spirit of Inez, as a test to see how dedicated she was to taking care of the house. Carolyn also witnessed a couple of strange occurrences in the entryway of the house. The fireplace screen and umbrella stand crashed to the floor by themselves.

There have been many unexplained paranormal reports from guests and employees. An employee named Chanity has experienced many strange things while working at the inn. One day, Chanity heard a sound like glass falling by the hallway leading to the kitchen. When she went to see what the noise was, nothing was broken. Another morning Chanity was all alone, setting the dining room tables for breakfast, when she heard someone sit in one of the wicker chairs by the linen closet. No living person was sitting there, but the chair continued to creak. However, the most prominent event that stands out in Chanity's mind was the day that she was showing a guest to his room. Someone had grabbed her shoulder so hard that it started to tingle...yet, when she turned around, no one was there.

Most of the paranormal reports come from the Magnolia Room, otherwise known as Mae's room. One spirit in particular likes to make her presence known through phantom smells and moving items in the room. One of the most common reports from guests and employees is the strong smell of flowers like lilacs that comes and goes. One guest who stayed in the Magnolia Room reported laying in bed and feeling mists of water come from the top of the bed's canopy. They couldn't quite explain where the water was coming from. Another guest stayed in the room for several nights. When she went looking for her pajamas, they were gone. Later, she found them folded and packed in the bottom of her suitcase.

Orb captured to the right of bed in Magnolia Room.

I had the chance to stay in the Magnolia Room, where I encountered some strange phenomenon. When I first arrived, I wanted to take pictures with my digital camera. I had just put in new batteries, but within minutes the batteries were completely drained. I had to drive for several miles to purchase new batteries. The draining of batteries is not an uncommon phenomenon when dealing with the paranormal, but there were other strange things that happened in the room.

Later in the afternoon, I was working on my laptop and using the wireless Internet. I didn't have a problem with the Internet connection until that night when I wanted to watch television on my computer. I was watching the show *Ghost Hunters* when I got disconnected. I couldn't connect to the Internet at all after that. I tried the Internet connection in the morning, but it was disconnected time and time again. When I told Carolyn about the problem with the Internet, she had no explanation for it. She thought the occurrence might have been caused by the spirit of Inez, testing my patience. I wasn't sure if this was truly paranormal until I had a conversation about my experience with the owner of the Magnolia Plantation in Gainesville.

Cindy, the owner of the Magnolia Plantation, told me that her mother-in-law stayed at the Herlong Mansion and had some unusual things happen to her. She stated that her mother-in-law loved television so much that she brought her portable with her just in case the inn didn't have one. When she plugged the television into the wall, she was able to watch it for a few minutes before it stopped working. She put new batteries in, but it still wouldn't work. She had to drive several miles out of town to buy new batteries and still...her television wouldn't work. She couldn't explain the malfunction and gave up on the idea of watching television while at the inn. When she returned home, she checked the television and the batteries and they were both working fine. Maybe the spirit of Inez makes her presence known by draining electronic devices or, in extreme cases, maybe she's resisting technology and just doesn't like people watching television in her house.

Across from the Magnolia Room is the Palm Room that has also had paranormal reports. This room has been called the Brothers Room because the Herlongs' son, John Simonton Herlong, lived there. On one occasion, an older man came to the mansion with his daughters to celebrate his birthday. He wanted to investigate the paranormal occurrences in the house and try out his new EMF meter. He was outside the Palm Room when the meter spiked to high energy. The energy followed him from the hallway to inside the bedroom. There may be some residual energy lingering in the Palm Room...Carolyn has heard rumors that one of the Herlong sons shot himself in that room, committing suicide.

John Simonton Herlong gravestone.

I believe that I had contact with the spirit of John Simonton Herlong in a dream I had while staying there. I recall a good-looking young man with dark hair entering my room. He lounged around the room like he belonged there. He said that he would hang out with me while I waited for Mae. He also told me that I should go to the cemetery with him. In my dream, we went to the cemetery in Micanopy and caught orbs on my camera. I didn't think much of my dream until the next day. When I awoke, I had the sudden urge to go for a walk to find the cemetery. Some mysterious force led me to the Herlong family plot. I found John Simonton Herlong's grave with his birth date of December 12, 1903, and death date of May 22, 1941. I then realized that the dream was a way of John reaching out to me to discover his death. I was unable to find out what may have caused him to die at age 41. Like so many spirits that linger, they just want to be heard and recognized.

The other guest rooms may hold memories and energy of the Herlong family as well. In the original house plan, dating back to 1910, the six children's rooms were on the second floor. The girls' rooms were on the east side while the boys' were on the west. The Dogwood Room was their playroom. The Herlong Room was Zeddy and Natalie's room — strange things have happened in this room. This is where the bathroom pipes burst when Carolyn first moved into the inn. One guest reported the high window in the bathroom unlatching itself and opening. They couldn't explain how this could happen since you would have to stand on the bathtub to open the window.

One unknown apparition that has been seen several times in and around the inn is that of an older woman with a shawl around her head. A framed picture that meets the description of the woman hangs in the second floor hallway. A paranormal investigation team that came to the Herlong Mansion stayed on the second floor, in the Rose Room. One team member took a series of consecutive pictures out the bedroom window. In one of the frames, she captured the apparition of a woman on the grounds with a stark face and shawl over her head. This same apparition has also been seen by guests on the second-story veranda. Guests have also witnessed rocking chairs on the veranda rocking by themselves.

The Herlong Mansion is truly a treasure in the small town of Micanopy. Within its grandeur, there is a house full of family memories, mysteries, and unexplained phenomena. The home even features a mysterious brick room under the house, thought to be a room for the Underground Railroad. An untouched hidden jewel can be seen behind the house — an original water tower, built by Zeddy in 1910, still stands today, overgrown with ivy.

Gainesville

The Gainesville area has been inhabited by the Alachua, Potano, and Timucua Native Americans. Spanish colonists began cattle ranching in the Payne's Prairie area using Timucua labor. The Seminole tribe settled in the region in the eighteenth century.

Gainesville was named after General Edmund P. Gaines, commander of U.S. army troops in the Second Seminole War. The town was established in 1853 as a result of the Florida Railroad Company's expansion from Cedar Key to Fernandina Beach.

Gainesville was the scene of small-scale fighting during the Civil War. On August 17, 1864, the Florida Cavalry drove out three hundred Union troops occupying the city in the Battle of Gainesville.

After the war, Gainesville encouraged freed slaves to settle there by establishing schools and churches. Gainesville experienced many changes when the University of Florida was created there by the Florida Legislature in 1905.

Gainesville's Haunted Sites

Magnolia Plantation
ADDRESS: 309 SE Seventh Street
Gainesville, FL 32601
PHONE: 352-375-6653
WEBSITE: www.magnoliabnb.com

The Magnolia Plantation was built in 1885 by Dudley and Melinza Williams. The woodwork, original to the house, was built by Dudley. The house became known as the Baird Mansion after Emmett Baird, who owned and lived in the house for seventy years. A legend has been passed down through the years about Emmett Baird, who was thought to have found a treasure chest belonging to Black Caesar, Billy Rogers, Jose Gaspar, and John La Fite at Fowlers Bluff, on the Suwannee River, in the late 1800s. Legend has it that he used his treasure to make his fortune and purchase the house. People have speculated that the remains of the treasure were buried in this house before he died in the 1920s.

From the late 1960s to 1990, the house was occupied by various groups, including hippies, college students, and squatters. The mansion became a party house and went through a state of disrepair for thirty years before being purchased by Cindy and Joe Montalto in 1990. Cindy immediately knew that she wanted to become an innkeeper after visiting her first bed and breakfast in the 1980s, so she and Joe sold their house in Orlando and went back to Gainesville to look for an inn. They contacted a historic preservation officer who showed them the Baird Mansion. Although it was currently off the market, Joe knew immediately that this house was the one they wanted to buy and made the owners an offer that they couldn't refuse. The renovation took 120 days to complete. It took a lot of hard work and love to turn the Magnolia Plantation Bed and Breakfast into what it is today.

The paranormal activity started when Cindy and Joe began to remodel the house. They slept in what is now the laundry room while the renovations took place. They worked around-the-clock restoring the house. Cindy started collecting antiques and books to decorate the house. She stored the items on the third floor. One day, when Cindy went to the third floor to look through some of the books, she heard a woman's voice say, "I like your taste in books." Cindy didn't quite know what to think about the phantom voice. Joe also noticed strange things occurring in the house. One day he said to Cindy, "I know there's something going on in this house."

Strange things continued to occur for Cindy. One night, Cindy had a dream of a woman materializing and repeating a name over and over to her. She was unable to remember the peculiar name when she awoke, though she was able to recall that the woman from her dream was elderly, wore old lace-up shoes, a black dress, a pearl necklace, and had her hair in a bun.

Over the years, several people who had lived in the house began to surface and describe a similar female apparition. Alec, a college student who had lived in the house, came to help Cindy remodel the mansion. Alec was staying in what is now the Azalea Room when he started experiencing strange things at night. After staying awhile, he decided to ask Cindy if she heard things in the night or saw people walking around. Jason, another previous tenant, was staying in the Gardenia Room when he saw someone walk up the staircase when no one else was in the house. He later described seeing the exact elderly woman from Cindy's dream. Another worker, Denny, was alone painting the second floor around four in the morning when he saw a woman walk down the hallway and descend the staircase to the first floor. The strange thing was that the apparition made eye contact with him and nodded. Denny nodded back as if nothing peculiar had just happened. He described the female apparition's appearance just as everyone else had.

Strange occurrences that relate to a female apparition have also been reported in the parlor. A couple of girls staying at the mansion were in the parlor when they saw a ghostly pair of shoes walk across the floor — there was no body. They described the shoes as old fashioned lace-up shoes.

The spirit of the elderly woman continues to make herself known to Cindy. One day, a local massage therapist who was sensitive to spirits came to the inn with a special message for Cindy. She told her that the elderly lady who lives in the house would show herself to Cindy, but she "knows that you're afraid." Maybe the spirit wants Cindy to be comfortable with her in the house. Cindy later came to realize that throughout the restoration process, the spirit was concerned about what was happening to the house. Cindy discovered through her research that the spirit's name was Melinza Williams. She had originally owned the house. Melinza's love and dedication to the house probably saved the house throughout the thirty years of disrepair and vandalism.

Besides Melinza's spirit, there have been sightings of a ghost cat in the mansion. Cindy and Joe first experienced the cat when they were laying in bed in their third-story apartment. They saw a pillow next to them move slightly and become indented by an unknown presence. Cindy and Joe also owned three cats and said they would always go to the same corner of their room, right below the tower stairs, and look up as if something was there. Their Collie dog would also stare at the same corner time and time again. Were Cindy and Joe's pets sensing the unseen animal spirit?

When I stayed at the Magnolia Plantation, I happened to be the only guest staying in the main house. I had the chance to stay in the Heather Room, where I experienced a couple of paranormal occurrences for myself. I awoke in the middle of the night thinking that a cat was on my head purring. This was strange in that there weren't any guests or animals staying in the main house. Later that same night, I woke up to the television being turned on all by itself. When I finally drifted back to sleep, I had an unusual dream of a little girl trying to tell me a message over and over. The only thing I could recall was that the little girl was trying to relay a message about Melinza. I later told Cindy of my dream and she confided that a psychic had once told her that a spirit of a little girl stayed around her often. Was this the spirit of the girl in my dream trying to relay a message to Cindy? I believe that Melinza's spirit still wants Cindy to be comfortable in the house with her.

I also had an unexplained occurrence happen on the first floor of the mansion. I had been working at the kitchen table until 9:30 in the evening. After I was done, I turned out all the lights on the first floor and went for a walk downtown. When I returned to the house around 11:30 that night, all the lights on the first floor were on, including the table lamps. I was the only guest staying in the main house, so I couldn't figure out why all the lights would come on by themselves. The next morning I asked the cottage guests and Laury, the caretaker, if they had come into the house and turned on the lights that evening. I found out the lights were not on a timer or turned on by anyone else that was staying in the mansion.

The Magnolia Plantation property also has six unique cottages for guests to stay in behind the main house. Next to the main house is a cottage called Ms. Huey's House. It was moved to its present location in the 1930s. Guests have reported seeing the house as a freed slave's house at a different time in history. While guests were sleeping, they dreamt of slave children sitting in dirt and a mother yelling at the children. Reports of a slave child yelling for its mother have also been heard.

Though Cindy tries to downplay the paranormal happenings at the Magnolia Plantation, there is definitely spirit energy surrounding the house and cottages. The spirit of the previous owner, Melinza Williams, and the ghost cat seem to love the house just as much as Cindy and Joe. While Melinza may have been looking after her beloved house throughout the years, it also seems like she wants guests and owners to be comfortable with her in the afterlife.

If you visit the Magnolia Plantation, you will definitely feel peace and love from the house, which has withstood the perils of time.

The Evergreen and Pine Grove Cemeteries

Buried in the Evergreen Cemetery are former patients of the Sunland Gainesville Hospital. Pine Grove Cemetery is very old and is thought to have been an African American cemetery with former slaves buried there. Orbs have been captured at both cemeteries at night.

Devil's Millhopper State Park

The park is named from the sinkhole's rounded shape. Fossils and bones were found in the bottom of the sinkhole. Legend has it that the mill hopper fed bodies to the devil. Screams and moans are heard from the sinkhole on the nights of a full moon.

St. Augustine

Saint Augustine, Florida, is the oldest continuous inhabited European city in the United States. It is said to have been visited by Ponce de Leon in 1513. Juan Menendez de Aviles established the first settlement in St. Augustine.

The settlers of St. Augustine have engaged in several wars with the British, French, Native Americans, and pirates through the years. Famine, hurricanes, and other natural disasters also took their toll on the city. In 1672, the Spanish built a military fortress named the Castillo de San Marcos to protect their interest from the expanding British Empire. St. Augustine was attacked twice by the British. The Spanish survived by laying low in the Castillo.

The British gained control of the city in 1763, though it briefly returned to Spanish rule in 1784. The Spanish, who had left during the British occupation, came back and tried to return the city to its former grandeur. The Spanish sold Florida to America in 1821 and left the city. St. Augustine prospered during the Seminole War of the 1830s and throughout the turn of the century. Henry Flagler came to the city and invested in St. Augustine's restoration and development as a winter resort. Mr. Flagler contributed some of the city's grandest architecture, including the Alcazar Hotel (now the Lightner Museum), the Cordova, and the Ponce de Leon (now Flagler College).

St. Augustine has preserved the sixteenth century Spanish colonial buildings as well as numerous historical buildings from the 1700s to the early 1900s. They can be seen in the old historic district's unique shops, restaurants, inns, and homes.

Ghost Tours

Ancient City Tours
A GHOSTLY ENCOUNTER
PHONE: 904-827-0087
WEBSITE: www.ancientcitytours.net

A Ghostly Encounter walking tour will entertain and inform you of ancient city haunts through the eyes of the theatrical Higginbothom family, who will serve as your tour guide for the night. Dressed in period costume and accent, Nicolas Higginbothom is one character who takes people, young and old, through the streets where "you will be stepping on the dead all night."

The tour first starts out at the Spanish Military Hospital (1784–1821). It is a certified haunted building, investigated by TAPS, Paranormal Seekers, and the Peace River Ghost Trackers. While it is a historical museum by day, it is a paranormal hotbed at night. Nicholas explains that the First Parrish Church of St. Augustine once stood on the hospital grounds. "They had to bury their dead out the back of the church, and onto Aviles Street, due to the yellow fever." With all the dead bodies, apparently there are restless spirits still lingering around the grounds.

Orb captured on table in Apothecary Room.

The first room of the Spanish Military Hospital is the Apothecary, where medicines were dispensed. Full-body apparitions of a man have been captured on camera. Electronic voice phenomena, in both English and Spanish, have been captured on a digital recorder. The next room is the Ward Room, which was used for patients' recovery. Patients were laid to either rest or die here. Beds have been moved away from the wall by unseen forces and artifacts have "jumped off the walls." The spirit of a lady has been seen in the corner of the room. Only children can see the apparition of a Spanish soldier in the room. While touring the room, people have caught orbs on camera and experienced bite or scratch marks.

While the "A Ghostly Encounter" walking tour covers a few of these paranormal occurrences at the Spanish Military Hospital, Ancient City Paranormal Adventures gives you the chance to investigate the hospital for yourself using scientific ghost hunting equipment. However, A Ghostly Encounter is a great way to see St. Augustine at night and hear about local folklore, history, and true ghost stories. You will hear about some of the famous stories, such as Catalina, a female spirit who haunts the women's restroom in Harry's Seafood; Chief Osceola, who was captured at the Castillo de San Marcos and beheaded by a local physician; and Andrew Ransom, the English pirate who escaped the garret in the plaza...only to wander the same area in the afterlife. Not to mention the spirit of young Elizabeth, who is the most frequently seen spirit of St. Augustine, at the City Gates.

You will also be told more obscure stories only the locals would experience. Most of the small shops along St. George Street and adjacent side streets have had ghost sightings and even unexplained dark entities. Along Treasury and Charlotte streets the Accent Shop and Casa Mesa have had "evil cross over into this world," according to Nicolas.

If you came to St. Augustine to see the dead, the most action is at the Huguenot and Tolomato cemeteries. At the Huguenot Cemetery, you will find several tours a night telling the famous ghost story of Judge Stickney, a spirit looking for his missing gold teeth. At the Tolomato Cemetery, four spirits — a ghost cat, Tolomato Indian, spirit child, and Bishop Vero — are frequently seen wandering the grounds.

Orbs are caught on camera all throughout the historic downtown St. Augustine and its cemeteries. Be sure to bring a camera on the tour, for you might capture something paranormal for yourself. A Ghostly Encounter walking tour is great for families and those interested in getting an overview of the spirits that haunt this ancient city.

Paranormal Investigation Tours

Ancient City Paranormal Adventures
PHONE: 904-377-7723
WEBSITE: www.staugustineparanormal.com

A PARANORMAL PROWL

A Paranormal Prowl is a one-hour walking tour with Tammy Chapman, a local paranormal adventurer. Tammy has been investigating the paranormal for eleven years. Her first paranormal experience happened in St. Augustine while on a guided tour of the lighthouse. She saw a phantom image of a previous lighthouse that had been swept out to sea. That night, Tammy and her husband had three more paranormal occurrences happen to them at the Castillo de San Marcos and while walking through St. Augustine's oldest streets. Tammy was intrigued with the paranormal from that day on and continues to search for answers to the unexplained.

Tammy's goal is for "others to have paranormal experiences that will challenge their perceptions of the unknown." While on tour, you will learn about ghost hunting equipment, protocols, and how to capture activity on film. Tammy will tell you some first-hand paranormal accounts around historic downtown St. Augustine and show you the best locations for ghost hunting.

Before the Prowl starts, Tammy shows the tour group what paranormal activity looks like on camera. She has a binder filled with pictures she and her fellow paranormal adventurers have taken. Many pictures contain orbs of spirits at the Spanish Military Hospital and Castillo de San Marcos as well as the side streets of downtown St. Augustine. Included in these photos are the incredible pictures Tammy and her husband took when they first started ghost hunting at the Castillo de San Marcos. They had captured "pillow forms" that resembled apparitions of children on the fort grounds. Later, while walking downtown, Tammy and her husband caught ectoplasm and an orb to back-up her husband's personal goose-bump experience.

Tammy explains techniques for taking digital photography of the paranormal. Main tips include being respectful to the spirits, being aware of your senses, and other outside factors that would distort pictures, but the key to taking great pictures is to take several consecutive pictures to back-up your paranormal experiences.

After you have been given some techniques and background on the paranormal, then you are taken to one of the best places to ghost hunt in the city — the Castillo de San Marcos. There, you will test your knowledge and skills like so many paranormal investigation teams have done before. Tammy's first EVP was caught inside the fort's powder room. She was inviting the spirits to join them when she caught a voice that asked, "Did you call me?"

Tammy Fyfe is a professional paranormal investigator and consultant. She often takes the "A Paranormal Prowl" tour to further investigate what she has already experienced at the fort. As a former member of TAPS, Tammy Fyfe has investigated the powder room as well. Not only has she heard voices and cannon fire, but she was also pushed while on investigation. While a lot of paranormal activity has been caught inside the fort, the grounds are extremely active as well. The best part is that you are free to explore the grounds up until midnight.

Orb captured to the right of drawbridge at Fort Castillo de San Marcos.

There are several great spots for catching activity outside the fort. On tour, you are taken to these hotspots around the walls and bridges, where temperature changes and camera malfunctions have occurred. Around the fort grounds, you might even catch the exterior lights going on and off by themselves, at will, without any motion sensors.

Everyone on tour gets a chance to test out what they have learned about electromagnetic field detectors and digital cameras. Several members of my group caught orbs on camera while three members, including myself, experienced camera battery drainage and camera malfunctions.

One final word of advice that Tammy gives is that "when you are ready to leave an area is when you should expect the most activity." With this in mind, a member of the group took one last picture under the bridge and caught what looks like an apparition's foot beginning to appear. When I later reviewed my voice recorder, I caught an electronic voice phenomenon at the moment we showed the guest's image to Tammy. When she claimed it was an apparition, a weird growling voice talked over Tammy's voice and said, "Snap them."

Castillo de San Marcos is a hotbed for paranormal activity inside and outside the fort. With the fort's history and tragic tales of death, you may be able to experience for yourself the spirits and energy that still linger here.

A Paranormal Prowl is a great tour for those wanting to truly experience the paranormal for themselves. You will walk away with a background in ghost hunting 101.

A PARANORMAL ADVENTURE

Investigation of Spanish Military Hospital

If you ever wanted to investigate a certified haunted location using your EMF detectors, infrared cameras, and digital thermometers, then this is the tour for you. You will be shown tips for catching paranormal activity and experience private time in each of the five rooms of the Spanish Military Hospital.

While the guides "can't promise that something will or won't happen," you are left to make conclusions based on your own experiences and the evidence you might catch. Tammy Chapman, one of the Ancient City's paranormal adventurers, explains, "Every investigation is a learning process. With patience and an open mind, you can open the doors to the paranormal with respectful communication." Tammy believes that spirits visit the hospital because people are open to their presence.

With that in mind, you will be placed into one of the five rooms of the hospital, equipped with an EMF reader, red light flashlight, and digital thermometer to confirm your experiences. Located in each of the five rooms are real-time infrared cameras. One of the tour guides watches for paranormal activity from the cameras on a computer located in the foyer. They will inform you, via walkie-talkie, of unseen activity in the room. The guides will also give you helpful hints about taking digital pictures, paying attention to your senses, and communicating with possible spirits. While you won't be told paranormal stories beforehand, the guides will go over your evidence and experiences with you afterwards to confirm activity.

The investigation I went on was quite active with paranormal activity. Everyone on the tour seemed to experience something.

My personal experience occurred in the most active room — the Surgeon's Room. I was sitting against a wall, facing the surgical table, when I felt a burning sensation on my back. I felt like the heat was coming from the wall behind me. When Tammy came to check on me, she confirmed my experience with the story of a girl who had felt the same sensation on a prior tour. The activity experienced by the girl was caught on camera. Another person took four consecutive pictures of a black shadow coming out of the wall with an arm reaching towards her. Tammy decided to take pictures of me, and we caught several orbs around me in the room.

Orb captured on door of Surgery Room, where the author is telling a story.
Courtesy of Tammy Chapman.

I have always felt a lot of energy from the Spanish Military Hospital. I feel that because of the history and emotions of the people who went through such trauma and pain, there had to be some residual energy left behind.

Tammy hopes that people on the tour learn to trust their instincts. "If one person has a personal experience, it is eye-opening, and soul-searching is bound to follow," Tammy says, adding, "If half the people who take the tour woke up the next morning questioning our existence, if they awake a bit more humble and respectful than the day before, if they woke up more inclined to listen to their instincts, well that would be a wonderful thing."

A Paranormal Adventure will give you the opportunity to experience a certified haunted building for yourself. You might walk away more enlightened and with a better understanding of the unknown. This tour is perfect for the ghost hunting enthusiast, as it provides you with a great environment and the knowledge and tools for investigating the paranormal.

St. Augustine's Haunted Sites

St. Augustine is said to be one of the most haunted cities in the United States. Because its history goes back to the late 1500s, the city is practically built on the dead. So many houses, hotels, businesses, and landmarks are said to have paranormal activity and ghost hunters near and far come to St. Augustine to investigate these locations. Nearly every local will have a story to tell.

City Gates
A spirit of a young girl who died of yellow fever near the gates has been seen dancing and playing around the gates between 2 and 3 a.m. Many orbs have been photographed here.

Castillo de San Marcos
One of the most frequently talked about spirits of the fort is Chief Osceola, who was captured and imprisoned here. After his death, he was beheaded by a local physician and his head was put on display in a local business.

One of the most active parts of the fort is the powder room. In 1784, Colonel Marti and his wife Dolores resided in the fort. It was said that Dolores had a love affair with Officer Manuel Abela. When the

Colonel found out about the affair, he had the couple shackled inside the gunpowder's chamber walls. This may account for the unexplained sounds of moaning and crying in the powder room. Sounds of cannon fire have also been reported.

The fort's grounds have a lot of paranormal activity as well. Spirits have been seen of a woman wearing a flowing dress wandering the grounds and a Spanish soldier looking for a lost ring. Many people have not only experienced cold spots, but they have also caught orbs around the whole fort.

Spanish Military Hospital

This building once housed the First Parrish Church of St. Augustine. It is said that dead bodies were buried in front of the building. The Spanish Military Hospital operated from 1784 to 1821. During that time many people died from sickness and amputations. People have seen full-body apparitions of a man in the Apothecary Room. Voices in English and Spanish have also been heard in this room. In the Ward Room, the spirit of a lady has been seen in a corner and only children are able to see the apparition of a soldier. People frequently experience hot and cold spots in the hospital and, in some rare cases, receive unexplained bite or scratch marks. The Spanish Military Hospital is a great place to take pictures of orbs both inside and outside the building.

Huguenot Cemetery

This cemetery was one of the original burial grounds in town and holds hundreds of victims from the yellow fever epidemic of 1821. The ghost of Judge John B. Stickney, who died in 1882, is one of the cemetery's most restless spirits — he sits on a tree limb or wanders the grounds looking for his stolen gold teeth and head.

Tolomato Cemetery

Four spirits — a ghost cat, a Tolomato Indian, a spirit child, and Bishop Vero — are often seen wandering the grounds and orbs are frequently captured on pictures here.

Old Jail

A former male prisoner who wears a plaid suit and hat has been seen and heard shuffling his feet inside the old jail. A large shadow of a male spirit, thought to be the first sheriff, Sheriff Perry, has been seen on the walls. Cold spots are felt in the cells and sheriff's office.

St. Augustine Lighthouse

This site dates back to the 1500s. The current tower and house were built between 1874 and 1876. According to The Atlantic Paranormal Society, or TAPS, the St. Augustine Lighthouse is the most haunted location in the United States. They even caught a full-body apparition on film looking down from inside the lighthouse tower.

There are several spirits that linger at the lighthouse. Two young girls who died from a railroad handcar accident have been seen in the lighthouse windows and innkeeper's house. Three male spirits have also been seen and heard in the innkeeper's house. One may be of a man that hanged himself on the second story while the other two reside in the basement. One is a large man who is a possible caretaker and is filled with dread while the other hangs out in the hallway by the cistern playing pranks on people.

Ripley's Believe it or Not: Castle Warden

Built in 1887 by William Warden, who lived there until 1925, in 1941 Marjorie Rawlings bought and refurbished the house as the Castle Warden Hotel. In 1944, a fire broke out on the third and fourth floors. Smoke killed two female guests named Ruth Pickering and Betty Richeson. Some say that foul play and murder was at hand.

Many people say there are several restless spirits that reside here due to tragedy and the various artifacts that are displayed within the museum. People report feelings of being watched, followed, and touched aggressively. Cold spots have been felt, and lights are said to flicker on and off by themselves. Items are constantly being moved around in the museum's gift shop.

O.C. Whites

The restaurant was once a private home owned by Mrs. Worth. Her spirit might still protect and look over the building. Employees hear footsteps on the second floor when no one is in the restaurant. Often the candles will light themselves on the tables. Doors have opened and closed by themselves and voices are heard. The kitchen is quite active with items being moved around.

Scarlett O'Hara's

The restaurant was once Mr. Colee's home in 1879. He was found dead in his bathtub from a possible murder plot. His spirit haunts the second floor martini bar and men's restroom. A spirit of another man has been seen and felt at the downstairs bar. Candles light by themselves and television stations change periodically.

Kenwood Inn

ADDRESS: 38 Marine Street
St. Augustine, FL 32084
PHONE: 904-824-2116
WEBSITE: www.thekenwoodinn.com

THE KENWOOD, ST. AUGUSTINE, FLA.

The Kenwood Inn started construction in 1865. In 1886, it opened its doors as the LaBorde Boarding House, run by Miss LaBorde and S.W. Cole and Sons. Rammond LaBorde helped run the inn during that time. In 1911, the Kenwood got its new name from Mrs. J. L. Morgan, who ran the inn until 1915. In 1915, the name changed to the Marine St. Inn. In 1920, owner Elwood C. Salmon changed the name back to the Kenwood Inn. Elwood managed the inn up until his mysterious death at the house in 1938. He also served as St. Augustine's City Commissioner from 1928–1930. The Kenwood Inn is the only hotel of its kind remaining from the Gilded Age. Pat and Ted Dobosz bought the Kenwood Inn in June 2008.

The inn has a vast history of serving guests throughout the years, with many unique characters having owned and stayed at the Kenwood. There have been several mysterious deaths at the inn as well. Paranormal energy surrounding the three spirits of the house, plus a ghost cat, is constant.

One lively spirit is named Rammond, after the original owner, Rammond Laborde. When Rammond owned the inn, he must have loved to entertain and host guests. He continues to do the same thing in the afterlife. Current owner, Pat Dobosz, is constantly yelling at Rammond for playing practical jokes in the house. Pat says that one day Rammond is unplugging lamps and moving furniture and another day he is stealing soap from the guests' rooms. A lot of activity from Rammond is also reported in Room 7, the Country French Room. Guests have reported lights and water turning on and off by themselves. It seems as if Rammond wants to make his presence known.

I have had the pleasure of staying in Room 7 several times. I have also had a match of wits with the spirit of Rammond on several different occasions. One time I was in the bathroom when the door opened by itself, leaving me exposed. I had to laugh at Rammond's sense of humor. Later, when I crawled into bed, I sensed a male spirit lean over me and whisper "hey" in my ear as if to get my attention. The room also seemed to get extremely warm that night. My husband and I kept pushing the bed covers off of ourselves, only to be tucked in again by unseen hands. The practical jokes continued into the next morning. I witnessed the long chain, used as a fan pull in the bathroom, spin in circles without any breeze or draft to move it. I immediately thought Rammond was up to his usual tricks, so I told him to stop moving the chain. To my surprise, the chain stopped moving completely. I was entertained by Rammond's presence.

However, the experience I had on the night of October 31, 2008, changed my views on the paranormal and inspired me to write this book. It was my encounter with the spirit known as Lavender that opened my eyes to spirit communication.

Lavender's spirit, described as having long dark hair, wanders aimlessly from room to room. Rumors were told that Lavender stayed at the Kenwood at one time and supposedly had an affair with a prominent doctor in the area. It is said that her heart got too involved and she threatened to expose the affair to the doctor's wife and others. It is rumored that she was stabbed to death in her sleep while staying at the inn. Room 10 is named the "Lavender Room." It is not known if this was really Lavender's Room, as Lavender tends to be restless, roaming the second floor hallways and rooms. Pat often finds long black hair in the Brass Room when no one with long hair has even stayed in the room.

My life-changing experience happened in Room 7 on Halloween night. I was in a deep sleep when I had an intense dream where I saw myself as a woman with long black hair. I had a vision of myself as the woman sleeping in the bed in Room 7. I heard faint whispers coming from two Spanish men talking to each other beside the bed. In an instant, I felt a dagger get stabbed into my chest. I could feel the intense pain and gasped. I was so startled that I woke up from the nightmare. I felt a weird energy in the room and listened quietly while my husband slept beside me. After about ten minutes, I heard footsteps outside the door. I then sensed a female spirit enter the room and stand beside the bed. It was less than a minute and the spirit left. I was astounded at what had occurred that night. I got a sense that this female spirit was trying to show me her death and solve her murder.

Another odd thing happened the next morning when I was getting ready to leave. It started out just like any other morning, getting myself and my six-year-old son ready for the day. My son was being playful and threw a pair of my socks at me. I was a little irked that one sock disappeared completely. It took twenty minutes and looking in every corner to find the sock under the middle of the bed. To my surprise, there was a stack of books under the bed with the sock. The books seemed out of place. Why would someone put books under the bed? I couldn't get this thought out of my head, so when I returned home, I had to call up Pat at the Kenwood Inn and ask her about the books. Pat thought that was a little strange as well. She had no idea why they were there or who left them.

Another time I stayed in Room 7, the books appeared underneath the bed again. I couldn't stop thinking about the significance of the books. Then one day it dawned on me that the books were a sign. Maybe the female spirit in Room 7 wanted me to discover her story and write it down. I proceeded to research the inn and write down my paranormal experiences in a journal — my journal entries became the basis of this book. I later found out by interviewing Pat that this wasn't the first experience in this room concerning books.

Pat said that two sisters were staying in Room 7 one night when they experienced a book being read by phantom eyes. One sister woke up in the middle of the night, only to hear the pages of her book, which was on the nightstand, being flipped through like they were being read by someone. The next morning, her book was on the opposite nightstand. The other sister denied taking the book and reading it.

After my experiences at the Kenwood, I decided to do some historical research on the inn. I spent a lot of time at the St. Augustine Historical Society. I found extensive history on the Kenwood Inn from when it operated as a boardinghouse in the early 1900s. I even found documentation in the city directory of a woman who resided at the Kenwood between 1924 and 1927. She was in fact a writer for the National Conservators of American Women. Could this be the spirit that likes to read the books? Maybe by making her presence known she wants to tell her story to someone.

Pat claims the most active spirit in the inn is Mitsy. Stories have been told of Mitsy, a woman who married a sea captain and stayed at the inn while her husband was away at sea. Mitsy would often wait on the second-story balcony for her husband to return. One time she saw his ship come in and saw him run into the arms of another woman. Rumor has it that she jumped from the second-story balcony, killing herself. Guests have spotted the apparition of an older woman wearing a full-length dress, wide-brimmed hat, and her grey hair in a bun, sitting on the porch looking out to the harbor. Most of the paranormal reports about Mitsy is the smell of her perfume...guests say that it smells like lilies of the valley.

Guests who stay at the Kenwood report a lot of paranormal activity in rooms 7, 8, 9, and 10. In Room 8, several guests have sensed a ghost cat. One woman staying in Room 8 on a cold Valentine's Day came downstairs in the morning all wrapped up in a blanket, complaining of a headache. The rest of the inn was very warm. Pat checked the thermostat in her room and it was freezing cold. The woman decided to take a nap and later awoke to an invisible cat walking on her. With her headache now gone and the room warm, the ghost cat seemed to ease her pain. Two different guests staying at different times have also sensed the ghost cat in Room 8. A couple staying in Room 9 — the husband was skeptical of the paranormal — reported a female spirit coming into their room at night. The spirit told the husband, "This is my room...Get out of my bed!"

Apparition caught in window of Room 7.

The Kenwood Inn is a perfect example of haunted hospitality. The rich history of the inn has served guests for more than 125 years. Spiritual energy has lingered from tragic events of characters that have owned and stayed at the inn. These spirits seem to reach out to owners and guests alike to make their presence and stories known. Guests have taken photographs of orbs all over the house. I even caught an apparition in the window of Room 7 when I was walking by the inn during the middle of the day.

The Old Powder House Inn
ADDRESS: 38 Cordova Street
St. Augustine, FL 32084
PHONE: 904-824-4149
WEBSITE: www.oldpowderhouse.com

In 1702, the property's structure had housed the gunpowder used by soldiers at the nearby fort. The Old Powder House once stood in an open field west of Cordova Street. In 1867, the building was torn down. The present structure, built in 1899, houses the inn and was run as a boardinghouse by Kitty Capo, her daughter, and granddaughters. Current owners Katie and Kal Kalieta were drawn to the Old Powder House in 1999. Although the inn wasn't for sale at the time, they made an offer that the owners couldn't refuse.

Katie's paranormal experiences began when she first bought the inn. Katie would work alone at night organizing things and one night she was in the kitchen cleaning things high on a shelf. She became dizzy and found herself falling backwards towards a counter…that's when she felt an invisible hand on her back pushing her forward, which ultimately prevented her from serious injury. Katie felt like something was looking out for her safety. She feels like the spirit that helped her is a man who may have died on the property prior to the house being built.

Conquistador painting hanging in Miranda Room.

Katie says that there's been a lot of paranormal activity around the back of the house, especially when they started to remodel the Grace Darling Room off the dining room. Renovation workers reported items being moved and displaced. When the work was completed, guests reported strange phenomenon in the room, including the fireplace coming on by itself and heating up the room to a sweat. One female guest even took a picture of a single small orb on the bed.

No paranormal activity was ever reported in the Miranda Room until seven years ago, which was when a painting of a conquistador was hung on the wall in the room. The painting was a family heirloom of a former guest. The guest had enjoyed his stay at the Old Powder House Inn so much that he wanted to give the painting to Katie as a gift to hang in his favorite room. The painting is said to have paranormal activity associated with it. When Katie tried to take a picture of it for the inn's website, strange images appeared over the conquistador's body.

Paranormal activity in the Miranda Room may be linked to the Conquistador picture, but other strange phenomenon has been reported to occur as well. One skeptical guest staying in the room reported activity from a spirit leaning over him in bed at night and whispering. He wasn't a believer until the spirit tried to communicate a message from the other side. Another guest experienced the bed vibrating for no reason. No one knows who this spirit could be. It may be possible that the spirit came with the painting.

Antique doll in Memories Room.

Katie is curious about the paranormal occurrences at the inn. Some of her questions have been answered by several psychics who have visited the inn over the years. She said her most prominent memory was when a psychic walked in off the street and told her, "Your spirits drew me here." The psychic also told Katie about a little girl spirit that was in the Memories Room and asked if Katie would like to contact her. The psychic sensed a little girl around the age of five, with long brown hair and a white dress, who had died of consumption. The psychic communicated with the spirit of the little girl, who told her to "thank Katie for the dolls." No one but Katie knew that she had bought antique dolls for the spirit girl to play with in the Memories Room. Katie wants the spirits in the house to be as comfortable as the guests.

However, the room with the most paranormal activity is the Serenity Room. There is a tranquil energy in the room, as well as some unexplained paranormal occurrences. Some people believe the spirit of the original owner, Kitty Capo, lingers in the Old Powder House Inn to look over things. She likes to make her presence known in the Serenity Room by keeping things tidy and the figurines lined up properly. In the room are two bronze giraffe statues. If they are moved out of place, they are put back in their correct position by unseen hands. If guests are messy with their shoes, their shoes are reported to be lined up perfectly in the morning. Guests' personal items often disappear for no reason, but are always found before the guest leaves or shortly thereafter.

Katie keeps a journal of comments from guests in the Serenity Room — a couple of the entries tell of the paranormal activity that has occurred in the room. One female guest wrote that she went to bed with a headache and woke up around 3 a.m. to a female apparition alleviating her headache. Another guest reported the armoire drawers being opened in the middle of the night and strange noises coming from the light. I had the chance to stay in this room overnight and I couldn't explain the bathroom light turning itself on at 3 a.m.

Katie says the activity happens regularly here at the inn. The spirits at the Old Powder House seem to look after the welfare of Katie and her guests. You will definitely feel the peace and hospitality while staying here. Katie loves the inn as much as the spirits do and believes there's nothing but "positive energy in the inn."

Amelia Island

Originally known as the island Napoyca, where Native Americans lived from the year 1000 to the 1700s, Amelia Island has been ruled under eight flags. French explorer Jean Ribault landed on the island in 1562, but was forced out by Pedro Menendez de Aviles in 1565. In 1573, Spanish Franciscans established the Santa Maria mission on the island. The area known as Fernandina was settled in 1685. British raiders destroyed the town in 1702 and left it deserted for many years. It wasn't until 1763 that the English settled there. James Oglethorpe renamed the island "Amelia Island" in honor of Princess Amelia, the daughter of King George II of England. During the American Revolution, Fernandina became home for English Loyalists fleeing the colonies.

In 1783, Spain again controlled Florida. A land grant became a plantation on the site of present-day Fernandina. The Spanish harbor of Fernandina became the nation's center for smuggling slaves, liquor, and foreign luxury goods. During the second period of Spanish occupation, the Patriot Flag of the Republic of Florida appeared as the fourth flag, but local efforts failed to take over from the Spanish.

In 1817, the Scotsman Sir Gregor MacGregor and a troop of fifty-five men captured the island from its Spanish defenders. They raised their own Green Cross of Florida flag, which became the fifth flag. The same year, after MacGregor had already gone, the pirate Luis Aury sailed with his armada of three ships into the harbor. Three days later he hoisted the sixth flag for the Republic of Mexico and declared himself ruler of the island. Fernandina became a pirate haven and location for buried treasure. Aury was run out of Fernandina by a United States Naval force.

In 1821, the United States took control of the territory from Spain. The American flag, the seventh flag, was raised. Fort Clinch was built to protect the harbor. In 1861, the Confederate flag was the eighth flag to fly over Fernandina. Confederate troops occupied Fort Clinch. A year later, a Union force restored Federal control of the island. After the Civil War, Fernandina became a bustling and thriving winter resort. This attracted such wealthy visitors as the Vanderbilts, DuPonts, and Carnegies.

Amelia Island's Haunted Sites

Williams House Inn
ADDRESS: 103 S. 9th Street
Amelia Island, FL 32034
PHONE: 904-277-2328
WEBSITE: www.williamshouse.com

Williams House Inn. *Courtesy of Deborah McCutchen.*

The house was built by Marcellus A. Williams in 1856. Marcellus Williams worked to survey Spanish land grants in the state of Florida. In 1865, he became the Registrar of Public Lands for the state of Florida. Jefferson Davis, a friend of the Williams' family, was a guest at the house on several occasions.

When the Confederacy took over Amelia Island during the Civil War, the Williams family moved to Waldo, Florida. However, the Williams House played an important part in the war when Union troops occupied the house and used it as their headquarters and an infirmary. When the Williams family returned to the island, the house became a safe haven

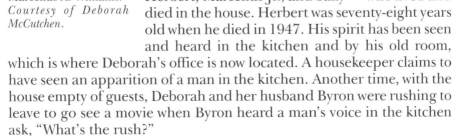

for slaves on the Underground Railroad. A secret room exists in the dining room behind the pantry door. The Williams family and their nine children occupied the home for more than one hundred years.

Owner Deborah McCutchen didn't give credit to the ghost stories before moving into the Williams House in October 2005. Prior to buying the inn, Deborah and her husband had stayed at the Williams House, but she didn't know it was haunted until she had stayed in the Egmont Indigo Suite with her husband. She had read the room's guest book in which people reported doors slamming by themselves and spirit children laughing in the room. Deborah laughed and told her husband, "We're not buying this house because it's haunted." After looking at more than thirty inns, they knew the Williams House was the right one for them.

Within a week of Deborah and her husband moving into the house, the paranormal activity started. Deborah was unpacking in the living room and placed a couple of tapered wooden candlesticks on the fireplace mantle. For a week, Deborah found the candlesticks on the floor, time and time again. She thought someone was playing a trick on her, but

then one evening, during social hour with the guests, the candlesticks came flying off the mantle and landed at the feet of some of the guests. The guests thought it had been a neat trick, but Deborah knew that it was the spirits' way of letting her know that they were there.

Another odd occurrence happened to Deborah while she was decorating the house for Christmas. She had all of her supplies of bows and pipe cleaners at a work station in the hallway. When she came back from decorating a room, she found her pipe cleaners missing. She searched everywhere, but she didn't find them until two weeks later — hidden under the dining room table.

Deborah thinks there are three spirits that live in the house: the Williams' children — Herbert, Marcellus Jr., and Sally — who lived and died in the house. Herbert was seventy-eight years old when he died in 1947. His spirit has been seen and heard in the kitchen and by his old room,

Marcellus A. Williams. *Courtesy of Deborah McCutchen.*

which is where Deborah's office is now located. A housekeeper claims to have seen an apparition of a man in the kitchen. Another time, with the house empty of guests, Deborah and her husband Byron were rushing to leave to go see a movie when Byron heard a man's voice in the kitchen ask, "What's the rush?"

Marcellus Jr.'s spirit also likes to make his presence known to guests. He died at age forty-four in 1912. Guests have reported seeing a man in a grey suit and fedora hat at the foot of their bed. Another time, there was a wedding at the house and guests were taking a series of family pictures on the front porch by the swing. In one of the pictures, there is a formation of a man standing by the swing. The man didn't belong to the wedding party and no one knew who this mysterious person was. Could it have been Herbert or Marcellus Jr.?

One of the most common spirits seen and heard in the house is Sally Williams, who died July 14, 1884, as a child. Deborah is among the many people who have had a memorable encounter with Sally. One day Deborah was in the living room, practicing a song for her daughter's wedding. While she was singing, the telephone rang and she went to her office to answer the call. When she returned to the living room, she heard a young voice singing along with the music on the compact disc. Other guests staying at the Williams House have also heard Sally. A previous owner of the Williams House has heard a child giggling outside the Egmont Indigo bathroom.

The rooms with the most paranormal activity include the Egmont Indigo Suite, King Ferdinand's Room, and the Veranda Room. Guests have reported lights turning on and off by themselves in the Egmont Indigo Suite. An apparition of a little girl has also been seen in the mirror of the room. Deborah says that the doors of a bookcase cabinet outside the Egmont Indigo Suite open and close by themselves.

I had the chance to stay in the Egmont Indigo Suite with my husband, Stan. I was having a restful sleep until I woke up in the middle of the night to someone tickling my toes. I looked around the room and noticed Stan was sound asleep. The next morning Stan told me that he kept waking up in the middle of the night, only to hear a child giggling. Was this Sally playing tricks on me and laughing about it? Sally's spirit can be seen and heard around the Egmont Indigo Suite, as well as the second floor hallway and staircase. Deborah says a guest captured a series of orbs on the staircase with her camera.

Meanwhile, in the King Ferdinand Room, guests have reported feeling like someone was watching them while they were sleeping. They have also heard something dragging on the floor. Deborah says she has "felt a presence" in the room when she's been in there by herself and knows that she wasn't alone.

Deborah and Byron never seem to be alone in the Williams House. She feels like the spirits have never left their beloved home. Deborah feels that "they loved it here, feel comfortable, and don't want to go." Deborah feels comfortable co-habitating with them, too. She always asks them if they like everything she's done to the house. "If they don't, they should let me know," she says. Maybe they didn't like the candlesticks on the mantle when she first moved in. Since then, Deborah has changed the candlesticks and there haven't been any complaints or activity from the mantle.

The Williams House is one of the oldest and most historic homes on Amelia Island. The spirits loved their magnificent home and apparently didn't want to leave in the afterlife. If you want to have a visit with the spirits, fall and winter is the perfect time. Deborah claims the house has the most activity during those months when the house is a little quiet. If you are the least bit sensitive, you might pick up on something paranormal.

Egmont Indigo Suite.

Palace Saloon

Though the building was constructed in 1878, the bar didn't open until 1903. During prohibition the bar operated with smuggled booze and a brothel upstairs. The bar is haunted by the former bartender, Charlie, who hanged himself in the building. His apparition has been seen in the morning hours. Beer taps come on by themselves and doors open by unseen hands.

Bosque-Bello Cemetery

The original section of the cemetery was founded in 1798 by Spanish Colonials. The cemetery is surrounded by live oaks and named Bosque-Bello after the Spanish word meaning beautiful woods. One of the oldest graves, from 1813, belongs to a French soldier who may have fought in Napoleon's army. Soldiers from the Revolutionary and Civil wars are buried here, as are Catholic nuns from France who founded schools in the area and helped yellow fever victims in 1877. There is an intense energy in the cemetery at night and several orbs have been captured on camera. When I was here, I felt like I was being watched.

Fort Clinch

The fort was built in 1847. Ghosts of Confederate soldiers and prisoners are seen around the grounds. A spirit of a woman in white has also been seen carrying a lantern. People have heard unexplained footsteps when no one else is around.

Amelia Island Museum of History (Old Jail)

Pirate Luc Simone was sentenced to be hanged at the old jail for murder, but he slit his own throat before his public hanging could occur. Today his ghost haunts the first floor of the museum where the old jail once was.

Chapter 3
Central Florida

Bartow ~ Polk City ~ DeLand ~ Cassadaga ~ Mount Dora

Bartow

Bartow was founded in 1851. The city's founding fathers were early governors of Florida, United States senators, and writers of Florida's State Constitution. Many military leaders also made their home in what was known as Fort Blount. In 1887, Jacob Summerlin, a wealthy cattle baron, donated one hundred acres to ensure that Bartow was established as the County Seat of Polk County.

Paranormal Investigators

Apollo Paranormal Investigations
FOUNDER: Cliff Kennedy
WEBSITE: www.apolloparanormal.com

Cliff and Lisa Kennedy started Apollo Paranormal Investigations (API) in 2006. Cliff had always been a skeptic of the paranormal while Lisa has had some experiences of her own through the years. This husband and wife team started out by investigating Fort Desoto in St. Petersburg, Florida, where they caught some amazing electronic voice phenomena. After that, they continued to check out other haunted locations in the area. Soon, they were getting requests from people to investigate their properties.

The goal of Apollo Paranormal Investigations "is to offer assistance to anyone experiencing unexplained occurrences and to document evidence of the existence of paranormal activity for scientific research." They go into investigations with open-minded skepticism as well as several devices, including a K-2 meter to pick up electromagnetic fields, a digital voice recorder to document any noises or spirit voices, and several infrared, still, and full-spectrum cameras to catch any movement or activity. Several members of the group are also sensitive to the paranormal. One such member is Psychic Medium Gemini Rose, who adds a lot of insight into the investigations, says Cliff. With her perception, Gemini helps them build a picture within a case. She is also able to help both the spirits and the living through her ability of clairaudience (hearing), clairvoyance (seeing), and empathy (feeling).

Apollo Paranormal Investigations has conducted research at some of the top haunted hotspots in central Florida and beyond. Among them are Fantasy of Flight in Polk City, Florida, where they created the NightFlight Paranormal Investigation Tour; the Ringling Home in Sarasota, Florida; and The Italian and Cuban Club in Ybor City, Florida. API has also conducted several investigations at the Stanford Inn, located here in Bartow, which has helped the inn's owner, Tony Grainger, confirm that the place is quite active with paranormal activity.

Paranormal Investigations

Fantasy of Flight

ADDRESS: 1400 Broadway Boulevard SE
Polk City, FL 33868
PHONE: 863-984-3500
BUSINESS WEBSITE: www.fantasyofflight.com
TOUR WEBSITE: www.nightflightexperience.com

Kermit Weeks, creator of Fantasy of Flight, had a vision of an interactive airplane museum where people could immerse themselves in dreams of flight, inspiration, and entertainment. He purchased the 300-acre plot of land in Polk City, Florida, in 1987. Around the same time, Kermit opened the Weeks Air Museum in Miami to showcase his collection of restored antique aircrafts.

Kermit had an overflow of vintage planes and was looking to expand. He wanted his second project, Fantasy of Flight, to be a larger than life experience. When Fantasy of Flight opened in 1995, Kermit had created two runways, Art Deco hangars, and two restoration shops.

The museum added 2,000 acres to its property. The Art Deco hangars contain forty historical airplanes dating from the 1900s to the 1950s. The airplanes range from the earliest flights to aircraft used in World Wars I and II. The museum contains the largest collection of vintage planes in the world.

Fantasy of Flight is known for its incredible interactive experiences. You can spend the whole day there experiencing all the aspects of the vintage plane's history, restoration work, and flight. You can peer into the lives of the men and women who have flown the historic planes by listening to the museum's audio tour and witness a vintage plane being restored in one of two restoration shops. At the end of the day, you can watch an aerial flight and demonstration. If you want to experience flight first-hand, you can immerse yourself in an actual flight of a hot air balloon ride or a vintage 1929 new standard biplane.

Ever since the museum opened, there have been occurrences of unexplained paranormal phenomena. The Director of Public Relations for Fantasy of Flight says that they have had paranormal accounts dating as far back as fifteen years ago. She says, "We firmly believe the activity is not from the location, but from the aircrafts." She says most of the paranormal reports come from employees who work early and stay late at the museum, though guests have also experienced such phenomena as unexplained voices and noises, movement, temperature changes, mists, shadows, and apparitions. Employees have even seen full-bodied apparitions near the vintage airplanes. An Operations Manager has seen a spirit under the left wing of a plane so many times he has started to speak to the spirit when he sees him.

In 2009, Apollo Paranormal Investigations heard about the Fantasy of Flight ghost reports from a customer of their day job and called Fantasy of Flight to see if they were interested in their team conducting a series of scientific investigations there. At the time of this book's publication, API has conducted three investigations there and with every investigation they get pieces of the puzzle to put together and draw concrete conclusions. Through their research, API had caught some amazing electronic voice phenomenon and evidence on film. The places with the most interactive activity are the Carrier deck, Officers Club, and Immersion area, as well as the World War Two B-17. Several voices have been recorded in the Corsair section of the Carrier deck and the Immersion area while loud knocks and noises are captured around the WWII/B-17 area. In the fighter town section, API has filmed orbs, haze, mists, and bright lights.

While API has investigated Fantasy of Flight several times, they wanted to share their knowledge with the museum and the public, so in 2010 they created NightFlight, a paranormal investigation tour. The tour is a hands-on investigation, open to the public, to further explore paranormal activity at the museum after-hours. Cliff says "guests at NightFlight have reported seeing things paranormal researchers wait years to experience." The more personal experiences and evidence of EVPs and video they capture, the better it is to help piece together a conclusion as to why paranormal activity occurs within the museum.

Apollo Paranormal Investigations continues to investigate the museum, along with offering NightFlight tours. API is concentrating on getting more evidence from the museum's most active areas. The carrier deck, which contains three aircrafts, produces a lot of evidence of electronic voice phenomenon and full-body apparitions. The room simulates the deck of the *USS Yorktown* aircraft carrier. A female apparition has been spotted in the room by a NightFlight guest. She describes an apparition of a woman with shoulder-length hair, wearing khaki pants, a beige shirt, and carrying a clipboard. Several other guests on a NightFlight investigation have been touched in the carrier area.

Three different women have said they felt their hair being pulled back on one side.

Cliff says that the room contains a piece of paranormal equipment called the Spira-Com, which is used in spirit communication. In the Corsair room, investigators asked if there were any spirits in the room and if they could state their name. A voice answered, "Melissa." No one knows for sure if this is the name of the female spirit seen or if there is history of the spirit attached to the aircraft. The only thing that API knows for sure is that the female presence has been constant.

A spirit with a British accent has also been recorded here on two of API's investigations. One time, when investigators were getting ready to leave the room, an EVP with a British accent was captured saying, "Don't do it," as if to tell API not to leave. Other scientific evidence caught by API in this area includes cold spots, scratching, knocking noises, and electromagnetic field energy.

During phase one of API's investigation, they interacted with a spirit trying to move a ball in the "Fun with Flight" area. A ball that was used as a demonstration was perched on its stand. Suddenly it fell. The team replaced it and asked if whoever did it could do it again. It fell a second time. They replaced it a third time and it was knocked off again. Another time in the Fun with Flight area, a female voice was recorded to say hi — and moan — in response to a paranormal investigator.

A lot of residual energy lingers in the Officers Club. The Officers Club is like stepping back in time to an airbase in the South Pacific in the 1940s. Cliff says that the Officers Club has been one of the most active locations at Fantasy of Flight. Cliff also says that a day guest of Fantasy of Flight contacted him a couple years back and told him that he saw an apparition of a lady bartender in the Officers Club. The spirit glanced away for a second and then disappeared. Several guests of NightFlight have experienced extreme sadness in this location. One guest felt like it was sadness from a broken heart — maybe this is the spirit's way of reaching out to people to make their presence known. It's still too soon to tell whether it's from the bartender possibly experiencing lost love.

The Immersion and WWII/B-17 areas seem to have residual energy as well as interactive paranormal phenomenon. When entering the Immersion environment, you will walk through an aircraft fuselage as you make your way to World War Two section complete with a replica battlefield from the time. There are simulated underground bunkers there also. While the Immersion Environment area was being investigated, a groan was recorded. Maybe it was from a spirit that had a war experience. Cliff says "that he can't think of a more emotionally charged area than the Immersion Environment...it's the ultimate sacrifice that was made by many soldiers that fought in these battles."

Next to the Immersion area is the room where the B-17 aircraft is kept. A lot of energy is associated with this particular airplane. Evidence has been captured several times inside and outside of the airplane. One NightFlight guest felt like he had unexpected heartburn while inside the plane. This was unusual for the guest since he rarely experiences heartburn. Other guests have heard rustling in the back of the plane when they were the only people inside.

Outside the plane, voices, shadows, and mists were captured on film by API. During one investigation, the API team heard voices of a group of women talking outside the B-17 room. When they exited the room to see who it was, no one was present. Another time, an investigator heard whistling and the "Amazing Grace" song being played. An incredible EVP was caught of a voice coming from a little girl in response to an investigator's question about a light being on before. The voice said, "Yes, I know there was one." Cliff says that one of the best pieces of evidence API has captured was a shadow moving down on the inside of the fuselage of the B-17.

According to Cliff, "residual haunting can occur in museums where artifacts may have an attachment." While there may be some residual energy caught at Fantasy of Flight, many paranormal reports have been interactive with guests as well as employees. As reported earlier in the story, an apparition has been seen several times under the left wing of the B-17 airplane by an employee. The employee says that it is as if the spirit is still working to get the plane flying again. During the day a guest reported talking to an older man in a flight suit inside the B-17. They said that the man in the plane answered some questions and was very helpful and nice; however, Fantasy of Flight did not have anyone working inside the airplane that day.

Other airplanes in the museum may have paranormal activity surrounding them as well. One time, API investigated the North and South hangars. Lisa and another investigator were standing next to one of the P51 Mustang airplanes. Lisa was trying to remember the name of the person who had owned the aircraft before Kermit Weeks. While Lisa was thinking, API recorded a voice saying, "Pauli." Paul Matz was a stunt pilot who had owned the P51 airplane prior to Weeks. Paul had been killed while making the movie *Flight of the Phoenix*. There is a possibility that Paul's spirit may still be attached to the airplane.

With every investigation that API does, the evidence they gather helps put the pieces of a puzzle together as to what is occurring at Fantasy of Flight. Cliff thinks that the paranormal activity may not be just tied to the land, building, or aircraft. He thinks the biggest piece of the puzzle is what Fantasy of Flight represents. Noting that many veterans and their family members have walked through the doors of Fantasy of Fight, Cliff says, "Who knows who they brought with them...Maybe some people brought spirits along and they liked the museum and decided to stay."

If you want to experience dreams of flight, inspiration, and entertainment, visit Fantasy of Flight during the day. While you will get a glimpse of the history of the vintage airplanes and those who have flown them, you may see or hear something paranormal for yourself. If you want to fully immerse yourself into investigating the museum's paranormal occurrences, then join API on their NightFlight tour. The tour lasts four hours and starts at 9:30 p.m. Reservations can be made through Fantasy of Flight's website.

Cliff explained that NightFlight is *not* a ghost tour but a true paranormal investigation. API won't tell you stories beforehand. All evidence captured will be reviewed. While there is no guarantee that you will see anything paranormal, it is an opportunity to learn the tools of the trade. Members of API will train you in the operation of scientific devices and techniques used by professionals to test paranormal phenomenon. The tour encourages open-minded skepticism while teaching respect for spirits and energies. "If you come with an open mind, you may leave with a life-changing experience," says Cliff.

Bartow's Haunted Sites

Polk County Historic Museum and Genealogical Library (Old Courthouse)

There were two courthouses built on this property, one in 1883 and one in 1909. In 1886, the Mann brothers were lynched by a mob in the street outside the courthouse for murdering Marshall Silas Campbell. Their bodies were displayed on the second floor of the courthouse for several days. Apparitions have been seen of their dead bodies and overwhelming feelings of sadness are experienced. On the second and third floors, an apparition of a lady in white has been seen. In the 1909 courtroom, people have reported cold spots and being touched.

The Old Courthouse is now the Polk County Historic Museum and Genealogical Library. On the first floor room containing ancient Native American artifacts, cold spots and malfunctioning lights cannot be explained. An explosion occurred in the basement boiler room, killing a male worker. Staff and visitors have heard screams coming from the basement.

Stanford Inn Bed and Breakfast

ADDRESS: 555 East Stanford Street
Bartow, FL 33830
PHONE: 863-533-2393
WEBSITE: www.thestanfordinn.com

This house was built in 1899 by prominent Polk County attorney Thomas Lee Wilson, who found success in his early twenties while investing in phosphate and citrus and working under President Wilson. Thomas married Cora Wilson and had a daughter, Tommie Lee-Meriwether. Cora and Tommie were known to host parties and entertain guests in their home.

Thomas died October 17, 1927, from a severe two-year illness. Funeral services were held in their home. Cora passed away not too long after. Tommie Lee-Meriwether lived in the house from 1908 to 1983. The house became an inn in 1995, after extensive refurbishment. Tony and Becky Grainger have owned the Stanford Inn since 2008. The Stanford Inn is known as the house filmed in the movie *My Girl*.

After buying the inn, Tony has experienced a few odd occurrences within the house. He says the house feels strange at night when he is all alone. He often feels a presence behind him when he's the only one there. He has witnessed lights turning on by themselves, but the experience that stands out most in Tony's mind happened in his upstairs bedroom at night while he was sleeping. When he awoke in the morning, he found a heavy shelf moved in front of the entrance to his closet. He could not explain how the heavy shelf moved itself — without any noise — while he was sleeping. Maybe this was a spirit's way of making its presence known to Tony.

Tony's unexplained experiences at the inn caused him to seek out scientific evidence to prove something paranormal was occurring in the house and so he called Apollo Paranormal Investigations to investigate. API founders Lisa and Cliff Kennedy, along with Psychic Medium Gemini Rose, investigated the Stanford Inn on three separate occasions.

Gemini Rose was able to feel the presence of the original owners of the house. She sensed the spirits of Thomas Wilson, his wife Cora, and an older gentleman related to the family. Most of the spirit reports come from Cora. Gemini Rose believes "the house was Cora's baby." While Cora spent a lot of time in the house entertaining, she also spent quite a bit of time alone while Thomas was away on business, causing her to become isolated and depressed with her life.

Many guests at the Stanford Inn have felt Cora's anxiety and depression in her old room, which is now the Cabbage Rose guest room. In particular, the closet in the room has a lot of energy and sadness surrounding it. Gemini Rose senses that Cora used to shut herself inside the closet and cry. Upon investigation, API received strong evidence from this room after they placed a wedding dress on the bed. At that time, Gemini Rose channeled the spirit of Cora and personally became irritated at what was going on. While this was happening, other team members received high energy readings from their K-2 meter. While breaking down the equipment for the night, team members asked Cora for any last signs of her presence. As they walked out of the room, they heard a loud bang on the closet door, which was recorded on a digital voice recorder.

I experienced paranormal activity soon after I checked into the Stanford Inn. After settling into the Cabbage Rose Room with a colleague of mine, we went downstairs to the tea room to talk with Tony and the API investigators. While we were talking about paranormal activity at the inn, an electrical rainstorm started outside. It seemed as though the energy from the storm fueled the paranormal activity in the house, as Gemini Rose started to sense a spirit presence around us. Soon after, she and Lisa heard a noise upstairs. Immediately, we all went upstairs to the second floor to investigate. While touring the Cabbage Rose Room, Gemini Rose and I both experienced a sudden sickness come over us while standing by the closet. When alone in the room, I felt like Cora would have cried at the foot of her bed for hours. I spent a lot of time that night channeling positive energy towards Cora. I even bought fresh flowers to display in the room, to cheer Cora up. Several days after we stayed at the Stanford Inn, my colleague and I were talking and she confessed to feeling a strong sadness that lasted for three days afterwards.

There has been a lot of paranormal activity reported in the second story guest rooms and hallway. During one investigation, Gemini Rose sensed an apparition of a woman in a white gown at the top of the stairway. The Francesca Suite is located to the right of the stairway. Guests report feelings of being watched, heaviness in the room, and a presence surrounding the corner desk. API caught evidence on their infrared camera of a figure of a woman in period dress. Cliff says that the IR camera is useful in capturing mists or materialization of energy.

The Azalea Room has had accounts written in the room's guest book about a male apparition seen in the bathroom. Gemini Rose believes the spirit to be a male relative or guest of the original owners. Several people have experienced an odd feeling in the hallway leading to the bathroom. On the tour of the inn, Tony pointed out that the hall closet, leading up to the bathroom, has a false bottom and was probably used to hide important documents or valuables. No one knows for sure whose spirit lingers in this room or why.

There is also quite a bit of paranormal activity that occurs on the main level of the house. The male spirit that inhabits the main level, as well as the master bedroom, is said to be Thomas Wilson. At API's first investigation, Lisa and team member Sonya caught an EVP of a male voice laughing after Lisa stated that she was tired. On their second investigation, Gemini Rose was alone, lying on the bed, when she sensed a spirit enter the room and stand next to the bed. Another time, Lisa felt a severe pain in her head while in the master bedroom. Gemini Rose associated Lisa's feeling as empathy for or pain from another person who has passed.

Upon researching the home and its owners, I found out that Thomas Wilson suffered a severe illness in the last two years of his life. His illness was never treated and he died while away on business in Atlanta, Georgia, on October 17, 1927. He was such a prominent figure in Bartow that his death was big news for the city — there was even a one-page article in *The Polk County Record* on October 17, 1927. The article also gave details about Thomas Wilson's funeral, which was held inside the house on October 19, 1927.

The house didn't always have sadness within its walls, as Cora Wilson and her daughter used to entertain guests often. In the Polk County Archives, there was documentation of a party for the Summerlin Institute's graduating class of 1910 held at Mr. and Mrs. Wilson's home. The tea room on the main level seems to have residual energy left from the many parties held there, and API caught an amazing EVP of wailing laughter and noises of people like they were having a party. Tony has also heard a lot of noise being made on the first floor between 4 and 5 a.m. when no one else is staying in the house.

There is quite a bit of documentation of the paranormal activity at the Stanford Inn — API has collected evidence in the form of electronic voice phenomenon, pictures, and personal experiences. The activity really gets stirred up when there is an electrical storm or special event happening at the inn. With everything that has occurred in the house over the years, there are great emotions left from the spirits who once called the Stanford Inn their home.

DeLand

Henry A. DeLand founded DeLand in 1876, with the purchase of a plot of land for $1,000. He convinced settlers to buy land from him and settle what is now Woodland and New York Avenues. The great fire of 1855 burned a lot of the original wood buildings, so they rebuilt everything from masonry. Henry A. DeLand built the present-day Stetson University in 1883.

Paranormal Investigations and Tours

Southern Ghosts
FOUNDER: Ray Couch
PHONE: 407-234-6611
WEBSITE: www.southernghosts.com

Ray Couch started Southern Ghosts in 2001 with a local ghost tour guide. Ray, who has always been sensitive to the paranormal and "wants to be a teacher to people," decided to focus on a tour that would show people how to investigate the paranormal for themselves. He says that paranormal investigating has "always been a passion" and that he was raised to "believe in ghosts." Ray experienced several paranormal occurrences while living in numerous haunted houses in Kentucky.

The goal of Southern Ghosts is to provide and coordinate the best paranormal event that one could experience. They offer weekend excursions and tours to some of the most haunted locations in the world, including Orlando and Deland in Florida; Gettysburg, Pennsylvania; and Savannah, Georgia.

Southern Ghosts caters to many different people and requests on a tour. Some tours last three to four hours while other adventures last two days for in-depth investigations. On each tour a psychic works with a group to direct them towards paranormal energy and teach them to be sensitive yet scientific when investigating. Though the tour guides teach people about the latest ghost hunting equipment available, they also encourage the use of simple tools — voice recorders, digital cameras, and a notebook — that everyone can work with for recording their experiences.

The first investigation Southern Ghosts did in DeLand was at the Artisan Inn in 2002. They were called to investigate the Artisan by a writer and restaurant employee who had some unexplained paranormal occurrences. When the writer showed Southern Ghosts the guest rooms, a psychic who was along for the tour made contact with one of the spirits residing at the inn. The spirit wanted to relay a message to Chryst, the owner of the Artisan. The spirit communicated that *they* have allowed Chryst to change rooms on the second floor, but won't allow her to make any changes to the third floor — or they will chase her out! When Southern Ghosts passed the message on to Chryst, she was surprised because she had just been discussing the remodeling plans of the Artisan Inn the previous week.

Southern Ghosts has done several overnight investigations and paranormal tours of the Artisan Inn. While on investigation they have captured electronic voice phenomenon, sensed intense energy, and found evidence of an unsolved murder of a prostitute. When giving tours of the inn, guests feel like they are being watched with some also reporting feeling terrified. When Southern Ghosts gives a ghost tour of DeLand, they first meet at the Artisan. Tour guests will walk through the inn and hear about its tattered past — and possibly even experience something eerie for themselves.

The second stop on the DeLand tour is the old Masonic Lodge, which was on the third floor of the historic brick building. The Lodge has the most terrifying stories in DeLand associated with it. While the building has been spiritually cleansed four times, nothing seems to get rid of the negative feelings and occurrences people have experienced there throughout the years.

While touring the building, I immediately was drawn to the only three windows on the top floor of the building. From the windows, I felt like I was being watched...and I could sense the negative energy there. Ray told me that behind the windows is where the members of the Masonic Lodge would get dressed and prepare for their rituals. Southern Ghosts has done investigations of the building, during which they have heard voices chanting and experienced physical contact and bad feelings.

Immediately behind the old Masonic Lodge, is a house that was DeLand's first funeral home. There have been several paranormal reports coming from the private home. Overnight guests would have nightmares and have to leave on several occasions. The previous owner contacted Southern Ghosts to conduct a paranormal investigation. They found cold spots, and experienced negative feelings.

There are several businesses along Woodland Boulevard and its side streets and alleys that have had unexplained paranormal activity throughout the years. The DeLand fire destroyed most of the original wooden buildings along Woodland Boulevard. Brick was used to rebuild them. Rob, a tour guide for Southern Ghosts, believes that the brick holds a lot of energy from the past. Businesses have come and gone throughout the years, but the energy and history have lingered.

Psychics and sensitives often feel overwhelmed by the energy from the buildings. Businesses on the tour include the Muse Book Shop, the Old Drug Store, Café Davincis, Architecture Antiques, Artist's Alley, and the Athens Theatre. At the time of this writing, several of these businesses were closed or have changed hands. If you get the chance to stop in one of these shops, you might encounter physical contact with a spirit, see an apparition of a spirit that used to work in the shop, or hear residual sounds from a business long gone.

While taking a private tour with Southern Ghosts on a quite Sunday afternoon, I was able to sense intense energy and receive images from several of the buildings. Along the end of Artist's Alley, there was an abandoned building that faced West Georgia Avenue. I immediately felt overwhelming energy and emotion. I sensed businessmen arguing and horse and carriages that could have been stored there. Ray later told me the history of horses along West Georgia Avenue: Antique Architecture, located on West Georgia Avenue, once housed a casket shop, where the owner had a horse and carriage. People have seen an apparition of a horse and carriage along the street. They have also seen the spirits of a little black boy and white boy playing in the street. Some say that the black boy had been trampled to death by a horse along West Georgia Avenue.

Ray believes that Architecture Antiques could hold energy from the pieces of old buildings that they sale there. Spirits also seem to be attached to the building itself, including the spirit of a little girl named Sarah, who has been seen in a white dress turning the bathroom sinks on and off. It is said that Sarah was the daughter of the casket maker who had his business there at one time. When Southern Ghosts investigated the east end of the building, they captured sounds of hammering metal on metal. During my research, I found a 1925 picture of Guenther's Blacksmith Shop, located on the 100 block of West Georgia Avenue, which might explain the residual sounds of hammering from the hard-working men of the blacksmith shop.

Southern Ghosts does everything to make a tour and investigation special and unique. During my tour of DeLand's haunted locations with Southern Ghosts, I had some incredible psychic visions and feelings. I even got the opportunity to see the Old Memorial Hospital and Museum and experience its paranormal energy for myself. I feel that members of Southern Ghosts are truly passionate about what they do and what they teach people.

DeLand's Haunted Sites

Artisan Inn

ADDRESS: 215 S. Woodland Boulevard
DeLand, FL 32720
PHONE: 386-785-1250
WEBSITE: www.delandartisaninn.com

The Artisan Inn was previously the DeLand
Hotel. *Courtesy of Chryst Soety.*

The Artisan Inn was opened in 1927 by Edwin D. and Jeanette Barnhill, but just a year later Jeanette died. Edwin claimed that his wife's spirit was haunting him by constantly telling him what to do and directing the operations of the inn from the afterlife. Edwin was declared insane the following year.

Later, the inn changed names to the Landmark and gained a seedy reputation, deteriorating into a state of disrepair. Reports of drug dealers and even a couple of dubious deaths occurred at the inn. Reports of prostitutes in the inn's basement were prevalent in the 1970s. According to newspaper reports from that time, a male guest refused to pay his bill for his extended stay in one of the rooms and was forced out by the owner with help from the local police.

The hotel was bought in 1985 by the Barnhill Corporation. It was shut down for eleven years, until 1996, at which time brothers John and Brett Soety became the new owners. The Soetys took on the task of restoring the inn. They also put in a restaurant. It took four years and a lot of hard work — everything from the original brick, wood, stairways, and floors were refurbished. They even salvaged the building's original doors, which are now displayed between the lobby and restaurant. The Artisan Inn is now owned and managed by family members of the Barnhill Corporation.

Chryst Soety, owner of the Artisan, doesn't go looking for paranormal occurrences, but she has encountered many strange things over the years. On several occasions when Chryst is closing for the night, she has seen a shadow down the lobby hallway or heard strange noises when no one else is in the inn. Most of the time, she goes about her business and rationalizes stuff away. Overall, she believes "there is something bigger than us all" that can't be explained.

Because the original Artisan Inn of 1927 was a retreat for snowbirds, the paranormal activity seems to be at its highest during the winter months, says Chryst. Paranormal activity also gets kicked up during renovations and repairs. The original hotel had forty guest rooms. In 1996, the hotel had to be gutted and reconfigured to make space for the restaurant, banquet hall, and other open spaces. Since the Artisan has undergone so many changes, there is a possibility that the energy from long ago still lingers today. Chryst thinks that "the building seems to retain the spirits in the bricks and wood."

Just about everywhere in the Artisan has had paranormal reports. On the first floor, the spirits like to displace employee items and move things to get attention. One jovial spirit likes to play practical jokes on the employees in the kitchen: one time an employee lost her watch...

only to find it later wedged under a 400-pound table. Customers in the lounge have seen wine glasses fly off the wine rack by themselves and come crashing to the floor.

There has been quite a bit of activity reported in the first floor lobby and hallway. Chryst's most memorable experience was seeing a shadow walking down the hallway at night when no one else was in the building. Also in the lobby hallway, two spirit children have been seen and heard playing by the elevator at night. One spirited girl named Amanda has been seen several times in the women's restroom. She likes to play with the stall doors. A customer even saw the girl's reflection in the bathroom mirror.

First floor lobby hallway.

While spirits on the first floor are a little jovial, the basement harbors the "creepiest feelings," says Chryst. An employee closing up at night saw a man wearing a fedora hat in the corner of the basement. Co-owner Claude has also seen a shadow in the basement. Other people have reported whistling, metal banging on metal, orbs, and cold drafts. Could the activity be a representation of the shady characters that used to conduct illegal business in the inn's basement?

The second floor of the Artisan has paranormal activity in the art gallery, kitchen, and banquet room. Local art often hangs in the second floor gallery. I got the opportunity to display my artwork here in June 2009. While hanging my work, one of the paintings next to me came up and off the chain by itself and crashed to the floor. I didn't know if this was paranormal at the time, but it definitely startled me. Later Chryst told me she had opened the gallery room one morning to find several of my paintings laying flat in the middle of the floor for no apparent reason. Often, when I went into the gallery, I sensed a sadness while looking out the window. While on a ghost tour of the inn, the tour guide mentioned that this room was originally Jeanette Barnhill's room. Could this be her spirit trying to have creative control over the room?

Various people and employees have experienced numerous paranormal occurrences while in the second floor banquet room. Paranormal investigators have caught electromagnetic field spikes and felt head trauma from spirit energy. People outside the building have seen a spirit of a woman in period dress looking out the second story banquet window. When the banquet room has catered events, employees have heard whispers and breathing in their ears while working in the second story kitchen.

If you want to experience the paranormal activity first-hand, you should stay in one of the third floor guest rooms. The rooms with the most activity are 1, 2, 3, 5, and 6. Guests report television channels and bathroom water being turned on and off by themselves. In one room, a guest reported seeing a refrigerator door open by itself and a bottle of water fly out and land upright.

Chryst says the most active room is #2. I got a chance to spend the night in this room and experience the activity first-hand. The room had an unusual feeling to it the minute I walked in. I sensed that something dramatic had happened on or around the bed. When I was in the room alone, I got the feeling that I was being watched. In the middle of the night, I awoke to a nightmare where a spirit was strangling me in bed. In my dream the spirit proceeded to drag me out of bed to get me out of the room. Chryst told me the next day that this may have been the room where in the 1970s a man locked himself inside for two weeks and had to be dragged out by the police.

In Room 3, guests have heard voices that have told them to get out. Outside the room, there is a red high-back chair that is said to be Edwin Barnhill's. A spirit of a cowboy has been seen sitting in this chair. Chryst nicknamed the spirit "cowboy" because of his thick boots, which have been heard by Claude walking up and down the halls when no guests were staying in the inn.

Chryst believes that the spirits are the "heart and soul of the building." The Artisan Inn has withstood many perils through the years. All the energy from the hotel's traumatic past, original owners, and guests have lingered within the Artisan's walls. The inn is a complete experience for anyone seeking the paranormal. Today, the completely renovated hotel hosts a full-service restaurant, lounge, banquet and meeting room, and eight suites with full amenities.

Athens Theatre

The building opened as a vaudeville theater in 1922. The spirit of a stagehand who fell to his death from the balcony is seen around the area. The spirit of a murdered actress who got caught in a love affair is often heard singing and laughing from her dressing room. Objects are thrown, the temperature changes, and moaning sounds are heard.

Oakdale Cemetery

In 1891, The Women's City Improvement and Protection Association of DeLand raised funds to buy the land on which the cemetery sits. The 1882 cemetery was known as Sylvan Park. The name was changed to Oakdale Cemetery in 1892. Many of the town's founding members are buried here. It is the largest historic cemetery in Volusia County.

Paranormal investigations have been conducted here. Several orbs, mists, and cold spots are felt throughout the cemetery. In the oldest section of the cemetery, unexplained footsteps have been heard and apparitions caught on camera. In the mausoleum section, where funeral services are held, a lot of strong energy can be felt. An apparition of a Spanish pirate has been seen in this area.

Cassadaga

Cassadaga is a small town in Central Florida that was founded by George Colby in 1875. Colby, a medium and spiritualist pioneer, established Cassadaga as a unique Spiritualist community in 1894. A native of Pike, New York, Colby attended camp meetings at Lily Dale, Cassadaga's sister community, in his home state. It is said that Colby was told during a séance that he would someday be a pivotal figure in founding a Spiritualist community in the south, and he later had a vision of a place with rolling hills and lakes. He arrived in Florida in 1875 with the help of his Native American spirit guide Seneca. Colby had come to find the place in his vision, which he named Cassadaga. He homesteaded the land in 1894 and deeded thirty-five acres to the newly incorporated Cassadaga Spiritual Camp.

According to local legends, Cassadaga lies on an energy vortex, in which the spirit and material worlds are uncommonly close. It is said ethereal vibrations emanate from the earth there. These vibrations are called ley lines. Psychics and paranormal investigators consider this area a hotspot for activity since it has the biggest geomagnetic vortexes in the country. Today, Cassadaga is known as the psychic center of the world. It consists of approximately fifty-seven acres, with fifty-five residences that make up a community of people who live, worship, and work in harmony.

Cassadaga's Haunted Sites

Cassadaga Hotel
ADDRESS: 355 Cassadaga Road
Cassadaga, FL 32706
PHONE: 386-228-2323
WEBSITE: www.cassadagahotel.net

The original building was a three-story wooden structure built in 1901. The Cassadaga Hotel was converted to a country inn in the 1920s. On Christmas night in 1926, the original hotel was lost in a fire. It was later rebuilt in 1928. Its romantic Victorian-style atrium, lobby, and deck are complete with piano and vintage furnishings. The Cassadaga Hotel was restored by the Morn family, who have owned the property since 1979.

Diane Morn owns and manages the hotel. She says that owning the Cassadaga Hotel "was meant to be" and maybe it was fate that delayed their flight back to Wisconsin in 1979. The delay led the Morns to settle in Florida and buy the Cassadaga Hotel, which serves as a spiritual retreat where guests can come to relax, take classes, and receive healing and readings, and people come from all over the world to do just that. At the Cassadaga, you can also communicate with spirits and receive spiritual guidance. It is a place where you can escape, reflect, and gain insight into the spiritual realm.

I am one of the many people who have been drawn to Cassadaga for spiritual purposes. My first experience came to me in a dream when I was thinking about writing this book. I had never been to Cassadaga or seen pictures of the town. I had a vision of walking around a quiet town, seeing historic houses, and being in the midst of an art event that lined the main street. I wasn't aware of the significance of the dream until I came to Cassadaga in June 2010 to interview Diane about the Cassadaga Hotel. After the interview, I went to the bookstore and the clerk noticed the handmade jewelry I was wearing. She suggested that I rent an artist table at the Cassadaga Family Days to sell my jewelry. I signed up and two weeks later I found myself in the exact scene from my dream. At the event, I met a fellow artist and tarot card reader who had set up next to me. She offered to do a tarot card reading, which shed some light into my personal and past lives. What I didn't expect was that this was the first of many visits to Cassadaga to work on my spiritual quest.

It was on my third visit to Cassadaga that I got to experience the peaceful Cassadaga Hotel and its spirits. When making my reservation, I had seen a room that I wanted to stay in on the hotel's website — it had a picture of an orb on the armoire. I envisioned myself staying in that room. When I arrived at the hotel to check-in, I was assigned to Room 2, which was the room pictured on the website that I had envisioned staying in. This same coincidence happened to three more guests who stayed in the hotel that night. Kat stayed in Room 3. She was surprised to find her room decorated with Buddhas since she is attracted to Buddhism and her lucky number is "3." Sisters Sally and Margaret stayed in Room 7. The number "7" was Margaret's lucky number. The coincidences made me wonder if the psychics working at the hotel intuitively knew which rooms to put us in.

Every guest comes to Cassadaga for different reasons. Margaret had been to Cassadaga three times before and wanted her sister Sally to have an experience there. Both sisters had excellent aura photos taken and tarot and psychic readings. Margaret said the minute she walked into the Cassadaga Hotel she could "feel its vibrations." While Margaret has never seen a spirit, her sister Sally just knows there is "something in the hotel." Margaret says that the hotel and town have such a "positive atmosphere."

Diane says the entire hotel is active with spirits. She feels that the spirits are all positive and feel loved and protected there. The spirits are most active when the hotel is full of people on the weekends. Diane thinks "the spirits feed off of people's energy." Diane has always known that the spiritual plane has existed. Often she will sense spirits standing around when no one else is in the hotel.

The hotel seems to serve spirits like it would regular guests. Diane says that a little boy spirit came to the hotel two years ago, probably with someone else, and decided to stay. The boy can be heard throughout the hotel laughing and playing with balls and ringing a bell on an old bike. A spirit girl named Hetta also likes to play around the hotel. Guests have reported someone playing with their makeup and jewelry. An employee at the hotel has witnessed the spirit children playing with dominoes when no one else was around.

I had an interesting experience concerning the spirit children. When I returned to my room for the night, I found that I had locked myself out. Luckily, the other door to the room was unlocked. When I fell asleep late that night, I had a dream about the spirit children playing pranks on me. In my dream, they tried to lock me inside the room by stacking chairs and tables against the outside door. I found them very mischievous and entertaining.

I wasn't the only one to sense the spirits in the hotel that night. Kat is from Chicago and she comes to Cassadaga every year. She admitted to feeling a little restless sleeping in her room the first night. She woke up several times to the feeling of her bed vibrating and a light touch on her arm. Kat admits to being sensitive to the paranormal. She sensed her grandmother, who had recently passed, was with her in Cassadaga. Kat shared with me several pictures she had taken of the hotel and the town. She had caught several orbs and an apparition of a man in the window of Colby Hall.

Kat and I both felt a lot of energy inside the hotel and we were both unable to sleep that night. I was in the lobby around midnight when I saw Kat with her digital camera wandering the halls. I joined her in taking pictures inside and outside the hotel. We were up until 1 a.m. talking about our Cassadaga experiences. While telling her about my book, we heard a voice of a woman that appeared to be coming from the hallway or outside. Kat went to see where the voice came from. No one was there, and all the hotel guests were fast asleep. While taking pictures of the hotel, I had noticed that an artist had painted a picture titled, "Lady of the Halls." Was this the spirit that was trying to communicate with Kat and I?

A spirit named Arthur has been seen by several guests over the years. According to Diane, he used to be an employee of the hotel in the 1950s-60s. Arthur also worked for the local newspaper and was known to be quite the comedian. In the afterlife, he likes to play practical jokes on guests. He has been known to answer questions and turn lights on and off. Visitors to Arthur's old room have smelled cigars and gin.

While several people come to Cassadaga to experience the spiritual realm, others come to heal and find direction in their past, present, and future lives. Cassadaga has been an important part of my spiritual journey. I have spoken to a few psychic mediums during my visits and even attended an experimental trance séance, which was definitely a new experience for me. I was able to feel spirit and human energy to its fullest. I also experienced what it was like to go into a brief trance.

Cassadaga is a retreat for the living and those in spirit, and the Cassadaga Hotel is the perfect place to relax, meditate, and experience the paranormal. The whole town is full of energy. On any given day you are apt to sense energy or possibly capture a spirit presence.

Lake Helen Cemetery

Two miles from Cassadaga is Lake Helen Cemetery. There is a legend of a Devil's Chair, which is actually a brick chair, located on top of the hill in the middle of the cemetery. It is said that the chair was designed by a broken-hearted man who lost his soulmate. In this chair, he would sit and spend hours with his dearly departed. People say that if you sit in the chair at midnight the Devil will speak to you about your wishes. Legend goes that if you offer him a beer he'll grant your wish. If you sit in the chair at midnight on Halloween, you will be held down. Many people have seen dark apparitions in the cemetery at night.

Mount Dora

Surrounding Mount Dora is Lake Dora. The lake was named after Ms. Dora Ann Drawdy, who settled the area in the mid-1800s. In 1883, Mount Dora was named after the lake. In 1887, twelve northern families bought 160 acres of land and settled there. Other important settlers were Mr. Ross C. Tremain, who was the first postmaster and a prominent businessman in 1891, and Capt. John Philip Donnelly, who became the town's first mayor in 1910. In the 1920s, Mount Dora expanded into a modernized city. In 1953, Mount Dora was incorporated into a city.

Mount Dora is now known as the "Antique Capital of the South." It's known for its festivals of antiques, boats, and art and crafts while the lakes of central Florida attract boaters and fishermen from around the country.

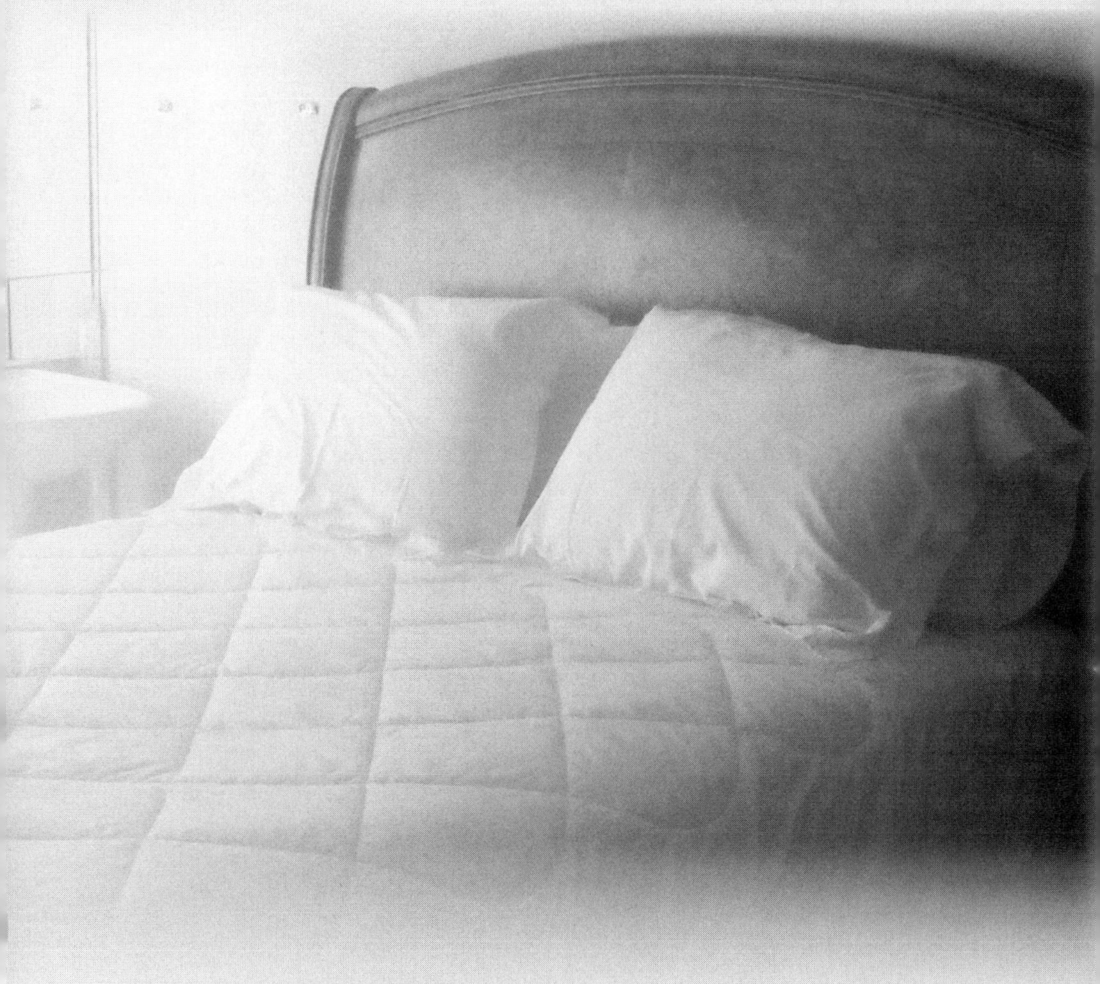

Ghost Tours

Mount Dora Ghost Walk
DIRECTOR: Andrew Mullen
PHONE: 352-434-1455
WEBSITE: www.mountdoraghostwalk.com

Started in 2008 by the Mount Dora Historical Society, the goal of the Mount Dora Ghost Walk was to raise funds for restoration projects around town. Andrew Mullen, former president of the Historical Society and founder of the Mount Dora Ghost Walk, helped gather historical stories, folklore, and paranormal accounts from archives and local business owners and residents to form the sixty-minute tour.

The Mount Dora Ghost Walk is now overseen by the Keyhole Society, a local theater group. They offer two tours every Saturday night at 8 and 9 p.m. The 9 p.m. tour is a special "steam punk" tour in which the guides dress up in Victorian clothes and act out skits along the walk.

Andrew Mullen, founder of Mount Dora Ghost Walk.

Both tours are geared around entertainment and are family friendly; however, you can also request an in depth paranormal tour with Jebidiah Ternbuckle, one of Mount Dora's resident paranormal investigators. His tour covers investigating with various equipment, including electromagnetic field meters, temperature gauges, and audio and night vision cameras. Any evidence collected is reviewed once the tour has concluded.

I went on a private ghost tour with Andrew Mullen and Jebidiah Turnbuckle. Jebidiah came equipped with his EMF reader, digital camera, voice recorder, and notebook. My private tour consisted of local folk lore and paranormal stories and evidence from several businesses and sites in downtown Mount Dora.

According to Andrew's research, one-third of Mount Dora's businesses and homes have paranormal activity. The Mount Dora Ghost Walk highlights the best stories from historic downtown and starts at the Lakeside Inn, one of the oldest structures in town.

The Lakeside Inn opened its doors in 1883 as the Alexander House. The original inn had two floors with ten guest rooms. It was a retreat for northerners, hunters, fishermen, and boaters along Lake Dora. Today, it has a total of eighty-seven guest rooms, a lounge, and a fine dining room. In 2010, the inn got a new owner and extensive restoration work on the buildings began.

The Lakeside has always had strange paranormal occurrences due to its lively past. Recently, with all of the restoration work being done, the occurrences have increased. Arriving at the inn, you can feel the energy of the guests and employees who once worked and stayed there.

The ghost tour starts in the lobby of the Lakeside, where you will be told the tragic story of a chambermaid who worked there in 1943. She fell in love with a butler who was staying at the inn. Only four days after they met, she heard that he had been involved in a fatal car accident. Some say she died of a broken heart after reading the butler's journal in a room in the Terrace building. Andrew brings tour groups to the room where the chambermaid died. People on one tour say they saw a reflection of the chambermaid's spirit down the hallway on the second floor of the Terrace building.

There are several spirits that still linger at the Lakeside Inn, including a little girl who drowned in the lake and a man who was poisoned in the speakeasy underneath the hotel. You might catch the spirits moving furniture or doors in the lobby.

Another stop on the ghost tour is the train depot of 1887, where you'll learn about Jonas Hatfield, who died by walking in front of a train. The story goes that Jonas was waiting for a train sometime in the 1930s.

Because of his faulty hearing aid, Jonas had a habit of looking three times before he crossed the railroad tracks. One day, he was doing his usual safety check when he was tapped on the shoulder. When he turned around, he saw an old friend of his, Mr. Buchannan. They had a friendly chat and agreed to meet a week later. He then crossed the railroad tracks without doing his usual check — and stepped in front of an oncoming train, which killed him instantly. Because of the tragic accident, it is said that Jonas Hatfield's spirit still walks the railroad tracks.

Just down from the train depot is Childes Park, the next stop on the tour. What makes this park special is that The Beatles stopped here, drank, and played music on their way to Miami. There have been rumors that John Lennon's spirit has visited the park. The town of Mount Dora treasures The Beatles' memory so much that an artist made a statue of John Lennon on a park bench and donated it to the park. Andrew said "if you kiss the statue's toes it will bring you good luck," so I immediately knelt down and kissed the statue's toes. Whether the legend is true or not, I did have a couple "lucky" things happen to me after the completion of the ghost tour.

Some people were not as lucky in life and died poor without next-of-kin in the town of Mount Dora. In the late 1800s, a red "X" was put on their bodies and given to Dr. Nutter to use their body parts. Dr. Nutter is the most talked about character on the tour. He used to work out of the Women's Hospital and had a private practice and domicile at what is now the Historic Mount Dora Inn. When Dr. Nutter moved to his second house (across from Childes Park), he built two additional coal chutes onto the house. It is said that the coal chutes were actually body chutes that led to the furnace under the stairs. One of the most horrifying legends of Dr. Nutter was that he once created a banshee-like creature consisting of one-third human parts, one-third animal parts, and one-third prosthetics.

Dr. Nutter's first house and office was in the 1893 Historic Mount Dora Inn. This house has some intense energy inside and out due to the horrific medical experiments and procedures Dr. Nutter conducted there. It is said that Dr. Nutter bought this house next to the slaughter house to mask the smell of dead bodies that he buried in the backyard and upstairs attic. Legends tell of a skull fused in a coquina stone on the property and the body of a pig fused on a tree in front of the house.

The legend of the "pig in the poke" came from Dr. Nutter's son Raspail, who confiscated the tissue and blood from a wild pig and body of a doctor that had been killed in a car accident in front of their house. Raspail used the tissue and planted it on the sapling of a tree in front of the house. If you look closely, you will see an unusual obtrusion growing from a section of the tree that looks like a pig's body.

Extreme paranormal energy still lingers at Dr. Nutter's original house. Prior to the tour, I had a dream about the house. In the dream, I was touring the home when I encountered the spirit of a very aggressive man inside. The spirit followed me throughout the house and backyard. The spirit wanted to attach himself to me. I saw this dream as a foreshadowing of what was to come.

When I arrived at the Historic Mount Dora Inn, I immediately felt a strong energy coming from inside the house. We walked through the front door to the foyer area. Andrew told me that in 2008 LSO Paranormal did an investigation of the inn and found electromagnetic energy in a particular chair in the foyer. When a team member sat in the chair, the electromagnetic field reader spiked to red for extreme energy. LSO also received high energy readings above a bed inside the bedroom attached to the foyer.

Haunted chair located in foyer of Historic Mount Dora Inn.

With Jebidiah on the tour with us, he did a base energy reading of the foyer. Everything was normal until I sat in the haunted chair. I immediately felt an intense warm energy enter my body. I was given the electromagnetic field meter. When I put the meter to the right of me, it lit up to yellow for increased energy. I continued to hold the meter and sensed a spirit energy right in front of me. The electromagnetic field meter continued to spike yellow above me. Soon after this happened we left the inn. The energy was still with me as I walked down the street. Just like in my dream, an energy had attached itself to me. As Andrew and I walked down the street, he told me that the foyer used to be Dr. Nutter's examination room. Does the energy from Dr. Nutter's patients and surgeries still linger in that room?

We walked from the inn to several businesses that have reported paranormal activity. The Blue Parrott is a restaurant that once was a hotel — in fact, in 1915, it was the first hotel established downtown. Its stories include the spirit of a little girl in a red dress that haunts the building. Both the girl and her father died in Lake Dora. The spirit girl now looks for her father's wing tip shoes underneath the tables. Across the street from the Blue Parrott is Piglets Pantry, where a ghost dog has been seen lingering by the front door.

The Renaissance is a beautiful historic building, that was once the Mount Dora Hotel. The building now contains several shops and the Frog and Monkey Restaurant and Pub. When the building was a hotel, a young couple staying on the fourth floor had a tragic accident occur. The husband woke up in the middle of the night to look over the banister. When he did, his shoes slipped and he fell down to the ground floor, dying instantly. When the wife saw what had happened, she leapt off the balcony in despair and died three days later in the hospital. The coincidence was that the couple was born three days apart...and died three days apart.

At the Renaissance, we stood in the very spot the couple had fallen to their death. We took electromagnetic field readings and digital pictures of the area. It is said that if you take pictures of the brick floor where the accident took place you might catch an outline of the two bodies. There is also a tale that if you go to the area that they died on a specific day, you will find rose petals there.

In the basement of the Renaissance Building is the Frog and Monkey Restaurant and Pub. The spirit of a man has been seen inside the bar. Employees have reported that inside the pub at night, globe lights would turn on themselves. When employees checked the lights in the morning, the globes would be unscrewed.

No ghost tour isn't complete without seeing a hanging tree. Mount Dora's hanging tree is next to Goblin's Alley. This alley has an eeriness to it, probably due to the energy and extra large vultures that frequent the area. The hanging tree was used in the 1820s–1840s as a form of frontier justice. The town leader of the time would hold full moon ceremonies at the tree, where people would have picnics and witness hangings. At the ceremony, five to twenty bodies would be covered in cloth and hanged from the tree. At midnight, the wind would blow the bodies around so witnesses could see the faces of the people hanging in the tree. Numerous orbs have been captured around this tree.

Legend has it that the tree is not a normal hanging tree, but an *intuitive* hanging tree: people have visions of other people who are going to commit crimes. Andrew informed me that the legend also has ties to a historical Norse legend.

The Mount Dora Ghost Walk and Paranormal Tour was extraordinary. I was told local legends and paranormal reports — and I got to experience first-hand some of these reports for myself. The energy from Dr. Nutter's house was incredible. The tour will definitely open your eyes to the paranormal while entertaining you at the same time.

Mount Dora's Haunted Sites

Fiddler's Pond

Outside the city limits of Mount Dora, along Donnelly Street and State Road 441, lies a deep sinkhole that settlers in the late 1800s named Fiddler's Pond. The settlers named the pond after a tragic event that happened there.

The pond was a popular watering hole for animals that carried wagons and passengers during the time. In 1875, the Warburton family was on their way to a fiddle recital in Eustis when they stopped at the pond to water their horse. The horse got too close to the edge and slid down the steep embankment — taking the family with him. The tragedy was discovered when someone found fiddle cases floating in the pond.

Some local residents have seen apparitions that wander the area late at night while others have heard sad fiddle sounds coming from the surrounding area. The horse is rumored to be buried in the Pine Forest Cemetery with the Warburtons.

Pine Forest Cemetery

The original forest cemetery consisted of two-and-a-half acres and was started in the late 1800s by J.P. Donnelly. The first known monument located here was for the Warburton family who met their tragic death in 1875 (see previous entry, "Fiddler's Pond"). The cemetery is now forty acres. Several orbs have been captured here.

Lakeside Inn

ADDRESS: 100 N. Alexander Street
Mount Dora, FL 32757
PHONE: 352-383-4101
WEBSITE: www.lakeside-inn.com

The Lakeside Inn was built in 1882 by Col. Alexander, Mrs. Stone, and Col. MacDonald and opened its doors in 1883 as the Alexander House. The original inn had two floors with ten guest rooms. It was a retreat for northerners, hunters, fishermen, and boaters along Lake Dora. In 1895, Emma Boone, an experienced hotel operator from Boston, renamed the hotel the Lake House. In 1903, the Lake House was renamed Lakeside Inn. An additional gatehouse was built in 1908 by George D. Thayer, followed by the Sunset Cottage in 1914. In 1924, Charles Edgerton and his son Dick bought the complex and built the Gables annex in 1928. Finally, in 1930, the Terrace annex was built.

The Lakeside Inn is on the National Register of Historic Places. Today it has a total of eighty-seven guest rooms and suites. The inn also features the Tremain Lounge and Beauclaire Dining Room. Some famous visitors to the inn have included Presidents Coolidge and Eisenhower, Thomas Edison, and Henry Ford.

The Lakeside is now owned by Jim Gunderson, who bought the inn during the summer of 2010. He had always wanted to own a historic inn and "fell in love with it." In December 2010, Jim began to restore, revitalize, and paint the inn.

Since Jim bought the inn, the work on it has been nonstop. With all the changes came an increase in unexplained paranormal phenomenon, which Jim claims "are all positive." Jim's first paranormal experience at the inn happened one night while he was sleeping on the third floor of the main building, where he lives. He heard a pattern of knocks on the wall that woke him up. The knocks continued in a rhythmic pattern and gave him a "weird feeling" that he couldn't explain.

The paranormal activity was a little more sporadic before Jim started to restore the inn. Most of the reports are from the many employees who have worked at the inn over the years. The most talked about story comes from a server who has worked in the restaurant for two years. One afternoon around dusk, the dining room was empty and she saw a chair in the dining room foyer spin, float off the ground, and land upside down. Later, after she put the chair back, it wiggled and toppled over on its side. She thinks that the spirit that plays with the chairs could be the spirit of a man often seen in the foyer between the dining room and lounge.

Another long-time employee has witnessed several paranormal occurrences at the inn over the years. While in the dining room one morning setting up for breakfast, she saw the doors in the service area slam open and closed by themselves when no one else around.

Beauclaire dining room.

She has also seen the image of a man out of the corner of her eye by the dining room foyer doorway. She almost felt like it could have been an "old manager making sure she was doing her job." Several employees say they have gotten the same feeling — that someone is watching them from the dining room.

A new employee has had a couple personal experiences where he sensed a spirit. His "chilling" experience happened in the kitchen while he was unloading a plate of dishes. He heard someone say "hey" right behind his ear. When he turned around, no one was there. Another time, he was in the foyer between the Alexander Room and the Beauclaire Dining Room when he was touched by someone tapping their fingers on the top of his head.

The Lakeside Inn has always been hospitable to guests of every age. In the late 1800s, it was quite common for families to visit the inn. Some of these family members are said to have lingered at the inn in the afterlife. A few people have seen the spirit of a girl around eleven or twelve years old in the main building. Wearing a blue dress and bow, this same spirit has been seen sitting at one of the dining room tables in the Beauclaire Dining Room. An employee was working at the front desk late one night when a couple staying in the main guest house complained that a girl was running down the hallway on the second floor. The receptionist knew the couple were the only guests in the hotel.

Another spirit girl named Amy, around age nine, has been seen gazing into the lobby fireplace. Andrew Mullen, founder of the Mount Dora Ghost Walks, tells the story of this little girl to guests on his tour. In 1892, there was a gala ball at the inn. Early the next morning, Amy was still in her red frilly dress playing near the lobby fireplace. She was waiting with her family to get on the early morning train. Amy saw her father, smoking his cigar, walk out towards the lake. She ran after him, got into a rowboat, and paddled out into the morning mist. She vanished on the lake and was never found. The strange thing was that Amy's father had passed away years before. People believe she was chasing his ghost. Some say that cigar smoke can still be smelled in the early hours of the morning in the hotel lobby.

With no prior knowledge of this story, I had experienced the smell of smoke when I came to the lobby around 7 in the morning. I thought it was odd that the lobby smelled like smoke since there was no smoking inside the building. Was I experiencing the phantom smell from the tragic story?

The main lobby is home to quite a bit of paranormal occurrences and legendary stories. When one receptionist started working at the inn in November 2010, she "never imagined that the inn might be haunted." Guests started asking questions as to whether the inn was haunted. The receptionist had heard stories from other employees before she started experiencing some strange things herself. She recalls one Sunday night she was working at the front desk and getting ready to lock up the lobby. She went to lock the Grandview Room door and returned to the front desk. After a while she noticed the door creaked back open by itself. After her experiences at the inn, she believes that "spirits exist." Another receptionist claims that all the spirits are "good spirits."

Andrew had his first paranormal experience at the Lakeside Inn. In the lobby, he saw the door to the tall chest open by itself in broad daylight. He had another experience while bringing a tour through the lobby at night: he saw a chair move by itself near the front of the lobby door.

One of the legendary stories that is unique to the inn is that there was a speakeasy underneath the lobby during Prohibition. Underneath the rug, in front of the reception desk, is a trap door that leads to a room below. This is where they used to hide the alcohol. There was even a tunnel underneath the inn to smuggle liquor from the lake. The speakeasy was a hotspot for gangsters during the Prohibition era. A spirit of a gangster wearing a cream-colored suit and fedora hat has been seen looking out the second-story gable window. Andrew thinks this could be the man who was killed by poison, poured from the bartender of the speakeasy.

Another spirit that has been seen in the second story of the main building is that of a man who stayed in Room 7302 during the Great Depression. It is said that he had lost everything and came to the inn he loved to end his life. Just recently a guest staying in one of the rooms at the main building reported that they felt someone sit down on their bed while they were sleeping. There have not been any reports of negative spirit activity at the inn. It would seem that the spirits that are here loved the inn immensely and have chosen to stay here in the afterlife.

However, the paranormal activity isn't just confined to the main building. The other buildings on the property have had their fair share of stories from employees and guests alike. Housekeepers have reported hearing noises, voices, and doors slamming when no one is in the buildings. One groundskeeper says that there is a lot of activity on the second and third floors of the Sunset building. He has heard voices upstairs when no one was in there. Another groundskeeper says that the door to the linen closet on the second floor constantly locks on its own accord. When he unlocks it and later comes back, it will be locked again. Sometimes this occurs as many as five times a day. The only known spirit to possibly inhabit the Sunset building might be that of an old manager named Bristol, who had a heart attack in the building and died in 2008.

A few paranormal reports have come from guests staying in the Gables building. Guests also claim to have strange dreams while staying there. One woman who was spiritually sensitive said she had a dream where a spirit family was standing at the foot of her bed. She described a heavy-set woman and a man with a child.

According to several members of the staff, the building with the most paranormal activity is the Terrace building. A bartender recalls a couple in the bar one day asking if the inn was haunted. The husband told the bartender that while sleeping in a room in the Terrace building he was awakened by the sound of a key jiggling in the door. He thought someone was trying to get in, so he opened the door...only to find no one there. While the wife slept, the man lay awake watching television. He said the same thing happened five times during the night.

Another time a different couple was staying in the Terrace building and the wife reported having a strange dream in which five or six spirits were standing around their bed. She said one of the spirits told her to leave. When she asked the spirits to nicely leave, all but one left — a spirit of a woman lingered in the bathroom, refusing to leave.

A receptionist at the front desk has had her own personal experience in the Terrace building. She was assisting a guest with a portable crib and, as she was coming down the second floor stairs, she heard laughter and talking on the first floor. When she arrived at the first floor, no one was there.

However, the most famous ghost story of the Lakeside Inn is a tragic love story of a chambermaid who worked at the inn in the 1940s. Andrew tells the story of the chambermaid on every ghost tour. The story starts in 1943 with John Hughes, a railroad entrepreneur, and his butler of forty years, Mr. Buchannan. They had come to Mount Dora to buy orange groves and were staying at the inn. One day while unloading a steamer truck at the inn, Mr. Buchannan and the chambermaid caught eyes. They instantly fell in love and for four days they were seen having tea together and holding hands.

The events that followed were truly heartbreaking for the couple. When Mr. Buchannan told the chambermaid that he had to go to Orlando on business for a couple of days, she cried at the thought of being apart. Nothing was more heartbreaking than when the chambermaid overheard the front desk clerk report that Mr. Hughes and Mr. Buchannan had been killed in a fatal car accident. On hearing this, the chambermaid fainted right on the spot by the front desk. Awakening, she immediately went to Mr. Buchannan's room, which was the first room on the second floor of the Terrace building. She sat on his bed only to find a journal of Mr. Buchannan's on the nightstand. She picked up the journal and read that on April 22, 1943, he planned to return to the inn, resign from his job, and ask her to marry him. Upon reading this, she fell backwards on the bed...and died instantly of a broken heart. An hour later, Mr. Buchannan returned to his room with a cast on his broken arm and found his beloved dead. The front desk clerk had heard the accident report wrong.

The chambermaid's and butler's heartbroken spirits may still be at the inn pining for each other. While conducting a paranormal investigation at the inn, Andrew caught an EVP at the location where the chambermaid fainted. On one occasion, when Andrew was telling the chambermaid story to a tour outside the butler's room, people saw the reflection of the chambermaid's spirit down the hallway. Andrew pointed out a photograph that was taken by a guest in the 1970s, which hangs on the wall outside the butler's old room. The picture is said to contain the ghost image of Mr. Buchannan. Perhaps because of the room's tragic history, it is no longer rented out to guests.

I experienced paranormal activity when I stayed in Room 7524 in the Terrace building. With all the lights turned off before I went to bed, I was awakened in the middle of the night by the nightstand light turning on by itself. I didn't realize until the morning that the light was a sign from the spirits that they are there too...wanting to be recognized and heard.

The Lakeside Inn is a perfect example of haunted hospitality. While there has been tragic events at the inn, some spirits just want to be seen and heard. Other spirits that roam the inn are nothing but good spirits enjoying the inn as much as the guests.

Chapter 4
Southeast Florida

Clewiston ~ Miami

Clewiston

The area beside Lake Okeechobee was once used as a fishing camp by the Seminole Indians. The first permanent non-native settlement began in 1920, when John O'Brien of Philadelphia and Alonzo Clewis of Tampa purchased a large tract of land to establish a town. They commissioned a town plan and built the Moore Haven & Clewiston Railroad to connect the community to the Atlantic Coast Line Railroad at Moore Haven. Incorporated as a city in 1925, Clewiston would become noted for its sport fishing.

Large sugar plantations were established around Lake Okeechobee. By the 1950s and 1960s, the cultivation of citrus, vegetables, and cattle were important to the economy in the area. The US Sugar Corporation is still the dominant manufacturer in Clewiston.

Clewiston's Haunted Sites

Clewiston Inn
ADDRESS: 08 Royal Palm Avenue
Clewiston, FL 33440
PHONE: 863-983-8151
WEBSITE: www.clewistoninn.com

Clewiston Inn.

The inn was originally built in 1926 by the US Sugar Corporation. It was destroyed in a fire and rebuilt in 1938. In the 1940s, artist J. Clinton Shepard stayed at the inn and painted a beautiful wildlife mural in the Everglades Lounge and Bar. In 2007, the US Sugar Corporation sold the Clewiston Inn to Big Lake Hotels. The new owners renovated the hotel and reopened the inn's restaurant.

Over the years, the inn's employees and guests have witnessed strange paranormal occurrences. Yandri, the front desk clerk, has witnessed several strange occurrences while working late at night. On one summer night when the hotel was empty, Yandri went to the lobby restroom around 3 in the morning. He recalls all the hotel lights being on dimmers to save energy during the summer months, so he thought it was odd that the women's restroom lights were all the way on and the men's restroom lights were completely off. Two hours later he went back to the restroom — only to find the men's room lights completely on and the women's lights off. There was no explanation for this as he was the only one in the hotel.

George, a maintenance worker, has experienced some "creepy feelings" while doing his daily rounds at the inn, especially on the second floor. He explains that the second-story banquet hall, known as the upper porch, has hosted various events, parties, and meetings throughout the years. When it is completely dark at night, George has to walk through the banquet hall to the boiler room. He says the room feels "eerie" and he often rushes through to get to the boiler room to turn on the lights and finish his rounds.

Second floor hallway.

When I was checking into my room on the second floor, my friend and I had to walk past the banquet hall. I found it odd that my friend, who knew nothing of the paranormal history of the inn, said as we walked past, "Don't ask me to go with you in that room!" I found her comment pretty odd. I later made her go into the banquet hall at night to face her fears. While in the banquet hall, we took some pictures and checked the room for any electromagnetic energy. Nothing paranormal was in the room at the time, but I could feel the energy of the room and envision events that had taken place there over the years.

The second floor of the inn is much like the banquet hall, in that eerie feelings are often reported from the hallways as well as the guest rooms. I wanted to experience the most active room on the second floor, which was Room 255. Upon checking in, Yandri told me he "doesn't like to go into Room 255." I later found out that a spirit in that room prefers to be alone. The first strange thing that occurred was when my friend and I entered the room. We noticed that all the paintings hung perfectly straight on the wall except one. The nautical picture by the window was slanted off its side. This normally wouldn't seem all that strange, except that all of the paintings had hard putty behind the frames adhering them forcefully to the wall. The crooked painting also had the putty behind the frame, but someone had purposely forced it out of alignment. With my friend's help, we had to force the painting back into its proper place. When I asked Yandri about the painting, he couldn't explain it being crooked as there hadn't been any guests staying in the room for a while. He said that often housekeeping would go into that room and report creepy feelings also.

Other odd things happened in Room 255 the night I stayed there. While asleep, I kept having nightmares about a male spirit that wanted us out of the room. In my dream, the spirit pushed my friend and me out of bed. I sensed that the room had been the spirit's room when he was alive. Another thing I sensed was that the hotel once hosted great parties, as it was bustling with activity in my dream. Neither my friend nor I could explain why we had trouble sleeping that night, as we were the only guests staying on the second floor. Other guests staying in Room 255 have reported foul odors and noises in the hallway or closet in the middle of the night.

Rooms 225 and 231, also on the second floor, have seen some paranormal activity as well. Room 225's reports stem from the spirit of a woman who passed away suddenly. In 1994, Mrs. Anita Conklin was living in Room 225. She was friendly with the staff and would ring the front desk every day. When Anita wasn't seen or heard from for a couple of days, the staff went to check in on her: she was found dead in her bed reaching for the phone. Months afterwards, the phone from that room would ring the front desk for no reason. This could not be explained because the phone jack in the room had been removed. Other strange occurrences are said to happen in Room 231, where a male guest is reported to have committed suicide. Guests staying in this room have experienced creepy feelings and cold drafts.

The first floor of the inn is also quite active with paranormal activity. Guests have reported seeing an apparition of a lady with upswept hair wearing a white dress in Room 118. She is seen standing near the vanity, by the window, pacing back and forth as if she is waiting for someone. Guests have also witnessed the lady brushing her hair at the end of the bed. She never communicates with anyone...just replays a scene forgotten in time.

Room 225.

Employees and guests have also witnessed paranormal activity in the lobby and kitchen. Employees working late at night have caught a glimpse of a gentleman in a brown suit standing near the lobby fireplace and they have heard the clanging of pots and pans and voices coming from the kitchen when the restaurant is closed. Wine racks have also been moved by an unseen force. In the dining room, some people have experienced being touched by a little girl.

Paranormal activity is not only present on the grounds of the Clewiston, but also in the guest cottages surrounding the inn as well. While taking digital photos of the inn at night, I caught several orbs on the inn's rooftop. Cottage 8 is supposedly haunted by a spirit who hanged himself inside. Reports by employees include a mirror crashing to the floor and pantry items being thrown to the floor by an unseen force.

The Clewiston Inn is an escape from the everyday hustle and bustle of South Florida. In the 1920s through the 1940s, the inn was used to entertain guests and executives of the US Sugar Corporation. Today, the inn has banquet and meeting facilities, as well as guest rooms and a restaurant. Several guests continue to stay at the inn in the afterlife.

Miami

Miami was first inhabited by the Tequesta Indians. In 1566, Pedro Menéndez de Avilés claimed the area around Miami for Spain and established a Spanish mission. During the 1820s, the Seminole Indians arrived to inhabit the land. In the 1830s, Richard Fitzpatrick was one of the first permanent White settlers and bought land on the Miami River to operate a plantation. Fort Dallas was built in 1836 on the plantation and functioned as a military base during the Second Seminole War.

In the 1890s, the United States government offered free land to settlers. William Brickell became known as the father of Miami. He held a trading post and post office at the mouth of the Miami River. In 1895, Julia Tuttle established citrus growing in Miami. She convinced Henry Flagler to expand the Florida East Coast Railroad to Miami and promote building and tourism. On July 28, 1896, Miami was officially incorporated as a city. Miami prospered during the 1920s, due to deregulation of gambling and prohibition laws and the land boom; however, it suffered great hardships during the 1926 hurricane and the Great Depression. In the late 1950s, Miami developed after World War II with the influx of Cuban immigrants. In the 1980s and 1990s, various crises struck South Florida. Among them were riots, drug wars, and hurricanes.

Ghost Tours

Ghost Tours Miami
DIRECTOR: Sandy Walker
WEBSITE: www.ghostgrove.com

A Miami local, Sandy Walker started Ghost Tours Miami in 2005. Prior to her ghost tour adventures, she was teaching theater in Miami's oldest playhouse. Her background in theater and storytelling was the perfect combination for pursuing the tour guide business.

Sandy's first experience as a tour guide started in Key West. Her interest in gathering stories led her to Key West to discover the town's history from old fishing families. Once she acquainted herself with the locals, she was recommended to Key West's original ghost tour. Sandy was hired on the spot. After commuting to Key West from Miami for three and a half years, it was only natural for Sandy to start a tour of her own in Miami.

Sandy felt "a lot of energy" from Miami. She started collecting stories from Miami's past and present to develop it into a two-hour walking tour that covers a half-mile. Sandy says that collecting stories is like finding treasures and she often "blends her personal history with the mysteries and old stories of Florida." Ghost Tours Miami is popular, so it is recommended that you reserve a spot through their website early.

During the tour, you will experience the energy of Miami's pioneer days, old Hollywood glamour, and tragic tales of murder and lost love. The tour starts out at the Coconut Grove Playhouse. The building dates back to 1926 and was converted from a movie theater in the 1950s. Hollywood's elite often frequented the theater for a music performance, play, or movie. Energy from the theater's glory days is said to have lingered in the building and one dressing room in particular is said to hold an energy vortex.

The next stop is Barnacle State Park, located on the shore of Biscayne Bay. The park reflects the natural Miami Hammock that once covered the city. The highlight of the park is the Barnacle House, which was built in 1891. It is the oldest residence on its original foundation in Miami. Here you will be told the story of Ralph Middleton Munroe. He was one of Coconut Grove's influential pioneers, civil activists, and boat builders. In the late 1800s Ralph sailed to the area and fell in love with the property and bought it. After the loss of his first wife Eva Amelia Munroe, who died of tuberculosis eighteen months after moving here, Munroe built and lived in the Barnacle House with his second wife Jessie Wirth. Ralph later donated land for the Coconut Grove Library to be built, with a stipulation that his first wife's grave remain on the property. Next to Barnacle State Park is Peacock Park. This is a good place to catch orbs and energy with a digital camera.

Ghost Tours Miami stops at the Coconut Grove Library, where you will be told of a gentle haunting that occurs inside. Sandy says, "In the years we have been guiding the tour in the Grove, we have developed the theory that the female figure that manifests at the library is a gal named Jessie." Sandy says, with an air of mystery, that the spirit cannot be Amelia Munroe. "When we visit her grave on the tour, you will discover why."

You may discover that a few businesses along Fuller and Grand avenues have haunting stories as well. One salon in particular has the spirit of a woman who died in a car crash and this spirit likes to make her presence known.

The most notorious stop on the tour has to be at the Mutiny Hotel. Built in 1969, the hotel hosted mobsters, Hollywood's rich and famous, and sports legends. Sandy tells of the hotel's checkered past through its "stirring tales of murder, betrayal, and steadfast true love." One tale in particular happened when a young beautiful hotel employee was murdered...her killer was never caught. It is also said that the top floor penthouse was used by gangsters as a surveillance room and meeting place. During this time, gunfire may have broken out on a few occasions in the hotel lobby. The Mutiny Hotel closed from 1985 through 1999. It was later refurbished and restored as South Florida's premier condo hotels.

Many times guests have experienced paranormal phenomenon. Sandy says that people "have been touched by invisible hands, photographed orbs, and seen figures that simply should not be present." Sandy says that she also has had "strange and touching experiences I cannot explain." She hopes to provide those experiences to her guests.

Sandy also hosts fireside gatherings, storytelling, weddings, and other events in a beautiful acreage of woods in a private location in Miami. Some of her unique storytelling includes a virtual Key West Ghost Tour, taking the audience through descriptive scenes, buildings, and streets of haunted Key West.

Sandy hopes to enlighten and entertain guests on Ghost Tours Miami. I feel that Sandy is a master storyteller who really gets into the role by dressing up in Victorian garb. Sandy doesn't want to give away all the good stories in print because she wants the reader to experience the mysteries of Coconut Grove for themselves. Sandy says that like "most of the guests who come on Ghost Tours Miami, you have to be smart, brave, and open minded."

Miami's Haunted Sites

Coral Castle

This castle was built by Edward Leedskalnin from Lalvia as a dedication to his long-lost love, Hermine Lusis. It took Edward thirty years to build the castle with simple tools and little knowledge of physics, astronomy, and geology. He worked in secrecy over the years, carving 235 tons of coral into chairs, couches, fountains, and pillars. He died in 1951 from cancer. Many people say that the castle was built on top of an energy vortex with Edward's supernatural powers. Many psychics have sensed energy, visions, and the spirit of Edward here. Visitors have caught apparitions on the property.

Coconut Grove Cemetery

The Coconut Grove Cemetery is known as the Charlotte Jane Memorial Park. There are over five hundred Bahamian immigrants buried here. Unique to this cemetery are the aboveground vaults. This cemetery became well known when it was used in Michael Jackson's music video "Thriller."

Paranormal researchers have experienced phantom smells that come and go, and the apparition of a man has been caught floating between vaults.

Miami River Inn

ADDRESS: 118 SW South River Drive
Miami, FL 33130
PHONE: 305-325-0045
WEBSITE: www.miamiriverinn.com

The main house of the Miami River Inn was built in 1905 by a German family named Elikofer. The main building operated as a hotel named the Rose Arms. The original hotel had twenty guest rooms that were rented out for $5 a week to vacationing New Yorkers. The Riverside community, in which the Miami River Inn is located, became home to prominent citizens who used the river as transportation until the Flagler Railroad was built.

Construction of the First Street Bridge in 1928 spurred the growth of Miami as a city, but left the Riverside community divided. The area became neglected. It wasn't until the late 1980s that Riverside properties were preserved and restored.

Sally Jude, owner of the Miami River Inn, was one of the pioneers for restoration of the Riverside area. She started her restoration work at the historic Warner Place. She saw how important it was to renew the community that started Miami and she is now part of the Miami River Commission, which works to buy and restore historic properties.

Room 11.

Sally had always wanted to start a bed and breakfast. In 1985, she sought to buy the Miami River Inn property from owners who lived in South America. It took five years to purchase and renovate the building; today the Miami River Inn consists of four cottages, with a total of forty guest rooms.

The Miami River Inn has several employees who run the inn for Sally. According to Sally, she hasn't experienced anything paranormal for herself, but she has heard several stories from her employees. One staff member has seen a woman in white around the second story of the main house. Other employees have heard unexplained noises and "felt like someone was there." Jane, who works at the inn, says she doesn't believe in the paranormal herself, but she has also heard stories from a few guests over the years.

Guests who stay in the first-story rooms of 11 or 12 have heard unexplained noises coming from the guests rooms on the second floor in the middle of the night, including doors that open and close, footsteps, furniture moving, and breaking glass.

I experienced these reports first-hand when I stayed in Room 11. Loud noises started coming from the guest room above Room 11 around 10 p.m. My friend and I could hear loud footsteps, shuffling, and something being dragged across the floor non-stop until 3 in the morning. All these noises continued throughout the night and left us wondering who was in the room above making the loud noises. I finally went upstairs around 3 a.m. to check out Room 21 — and found that it was completely quiet on the second floor.

The next morning at breakfast, we met a couple who was staying in Room 22. I told them about the loud noises coming from the second floor that night and asked if they had heard anything. They said they had just flown into town that night and checked into their room around 9 p.m. They were so exhausted from their trip that they immediately went to bed. They didn't hear the loud noises that we experienced. That morning, while checking out, I asked the front desk clerk if anyone had stayed in Room 21 the night before. He said no one had stayed in the room. Nor could he explain the loud noises.

The Miami River Inn is a standing gem in the historic Riverside community. With the inn residing in the oldest building in the Miami area, it is no wonder that energy and spirits have lingered.

Bibliography

Easley, Nicole Carlson. *Hauntings in Florida's Panhandle*. Atglen, Pennsylvania: Schiffer Publishing Ltd., 2009.

Jenkins, Greg. *Florida's Ghostly Legends and Haunted Folklore: Volume 1, 2: North Florida and St. Augustine*. Sarasota, Florida: Pineapple Press, 2005, 2007.

Karcher, Janet and John Hutchinson. *The Spirit Connection: Back to Cassadaga*. Deltona, Florida: Spirit Publishing, 2009.

Lapham, Dave. *Ancient City Hauntings: More Ghosts of St. Augustine*. Sarasota, Florida: Pineapple Press, 2004.

Ghost Hunting Florida. Cincinnati, Ohio: Clerisy Press, 2010.

Lewis, Chad and Fisk, Terry. *The Florida Road Guide to Haunted Locations*. Eau Claire, Wisconsin: Unexplained Research Publishing Company, 2010.

Martin, C. Lee. *Florida Ghosts and Pirates: Jacksonville, Fernandina, Amelia Island, St. Augustine, Daytona*. Atglen, Pennsylvania: Schiffer Publishing, Ltd., 2008.

Moore, Joyce Elson. *Haunt Hunters Guide to Florida*. Sarasota, Florida: Pineapple Press, 1998.

Powell, Jack. *Haunting Sunshine: Ghostly Tales from Florida's Shadows*. Sarasota, Florida: Pineapple Press, 2001.

Schlosser, S. E. *Spooky Florida: Tale of Hauntings, Strange Happenings, and other Local Lore*. Guilford, Connecticut: Morris Book Publishing, LLC, 2010.

Smith, Doris. *Haunted DeLand and the Ghosts of West Volusia County*. Charleston, South Carolina: The History Press, 2008.

Turnage, Sheila. *Haunted Inns of the Southeast*. Winston-Salem, North Carolina: John F. Blair, Publisher, 2001.

Index